# Essential
# Austria

### by Christopher and Melanie Rice

Since Christopher completed his PhD in
Russian History, he and Melanie have
travelled widely and have written numerous
travel guides. Their titles for AA Publishing
include *Essential Prague*, *CityPack Moscow*,
*CityPack Istanbul*, AA/Thomas Cook
*Travellers Berlin*, *Explorer Moscow and St
Petersburg* and *Explorer Turkish Coast*. The
Rices have also written more than 20 titles
for children.

Above: *Mariazell at its most picturesque*

**AA Publishing**

**Written by Christopher and Melanie Rice**

Published and distributed in the United Kingdom by AA Publishing, a trading name of Automobile Association Developments Limited, whose registered office is Norfolk House, Priestley Road, Basingstoke, Hampshire, RG24 9NY.
Registered number 1878835.

*Alpine dwellers blowing their own trumpets*

Front cover: *Innsbruck; Hundertwasser building, Vienna; national costume*
Back cover: *Cafe Demel, Vienna*

A CIP catalogue record for this book is available from the British Library.

ISBN 0 7495 2295 X

The contents of this publication are believed correct at the time of printing. Nevertheless, the publishers cannot be held responsible for any errors or omissions or for changes in the details given in this guide or for the consequences of any reliance on the information it provides. Assessments of attractions, hotels, restaurants and other sights are based upon the author's personal experience and, therefore, necessarily contain elements of subjective opinion which may not reflect the publisher's opinion or dictate a reader's own experience on another occasion.

We have tried to ensure accuracy in this guide, but things do change and we would be grateful if readers would advise us of any inaccuracies they may encounter.

Colour separation: Chroma Graphics (Overseas) Pte Ltd, Singapore
Printed and bound in Italy by Printer Trento Srl

Find out more about AA Publishing and the wide range of services the AA provides by visiting our web site at www.theaa.co.uk

# Contents

# About this Book

## KEY TO SYMBOLS

| | | | |
|---|---|---|---|
| ✚ | map reference to the maps found in the What to See section | 🛳 | ferry crossings and boat excursions |
| ✉ | address or location | ✈ | travel by air |
| ☎ | telephone number | ℹ | tourist information |
| 🕓 | opening times | ♿ | facilities for visitors with disabilities |
| 🍴 | restaurant or café on premises or near by | ✋ | admission charge |
| Ⓜ | nearest underground train station | ↔ | other places of interest near by |
| 🚍 | nearest bus/tram route | ❓ | other practical information |
| 🚆 | nearest overground train station | ▶ | indicates the page where you will find a fuller description |

**Essential *Austria*** is divided into five sections to cover the most important aspects of your visit to Austria.

### Viewing Austria pages 5–14
An introduction to Austria by the authors.
Austria's Features
Essence of Austria
The Shaping of Austria
Peace and Quiet
Austria's Famous

### Top Ten pages 15–26
The authors' choice of the Top Ten places to see in Austria, each with practical information.

### What to See pages 27–90
The country has been divided into four sections, each with its own brief introduction and an alphabetical listing of the main attractions.
Practical information
Snippets of 'Did you know…' information
4 suggested walk
4 suggested drives
2 features

### Where To... pages 91–116
Detailed listings of the best places to eat, stay,

shop, take the children and be entertained.

### Practical Matters pages 117–24
A highly visual section containing essential travel information.

### Maps
All map references are to the individual maps found in the What to See section of this guide.
For example, Kitzbühel has the reference ✚ 81E3 – indicating the page on which the map is located and the grid square in which the town is to be found. A list of the maps that have been used in this travel guide can be found in the index.

### Prices
Where appropriate, an indication of the cost of an establishment is given by **£** signs:
**£££** denotes higher prices, **££** denotes average prices, while **£** denotes lower charges.

### Star Ratings
Most of the places described in this book have been given a separate rating:
| | |
|---|---|
| ✪✪✪ | Do not miss |
| ✪✪ | Highly recommended |
| ✪ | Worth seeing |

# Viewing
# Austria

Above: *All the fun of the fair at the Prater, Vienna*
Right: *Tirolean folk costume*

# The Authors' Austria

## Heartland
One of the fascinating things about Austria is her genius for creating a distinctive national identity while readily absorbing the cultural influences of her neighbours. This remarkable gift was born out of necessity. Geographically Austria lies at the crossroads between western and eastern Europe while historically she emerged from the crucible of contending German, Slav and Magyar nationalisms. Austria has earned her place in the European Community of nations. After all, it was at the gates of Vienna that the inexorable advance of the Ottoman Turks was finally halted in the 17th century. Perhaps it's worth reflecting on what might have become of western civilisation had Vienna fallen.

*Tradition brings people together in communities like Hallstatt*

Think of Austria and inevitably it's scenery that springs to mind: the view from the train window as you cross the Semmering Pass, the cable-car ascent of the Pfänder overlooking Lake Constance, the ferry across the lake to Hallstatt or the exhilarating drive on the Grossglockner mountain highway. No wonder the Austrian landscapes have inspired so many composers from Mahler and Bruckner to Scubert and Johann Strauss – not to mention Rogers and Hammerstein (remember *The Sound of Music*?). Salzburg is also the birthplace of Mozart and the venue of the annual Salzburg Festival. Don't worry if you can't get tickets, there are dozens of other musical celebrations up and down the country and some extraordinary locations – the most spectacular being the floating stage at Bregenz, where the Bodensee (Lake Constance) provides the backdrop.

A popular misconception is that Austria is so steeped in tradition and the values of an imperial past that there's no room for youth and modernity. This couldn't be further from the truth. Take Austria's second city, Graz, for example, where one person in every six is a student – a factor in the location of 'Styrian Autumn', one of the most important contemporary arts festivals in Europe.

As a sports mecca, attracting enthusiasts from all over the world, Austria is second to none. Excellent faciliites and warm hospitality make it a first choice for winter sports enthusiasts, while in the summer you can try everything from rock climbing to river rafting.

As you'll soon discover, each of Austria's six provinces has a distinct identity, and the fact that its peoples are so diverse may come as a surprise. It's this variety that makes Austria so special: one country, many facets.

# Austria's Features

## Geography

• Austria lies at the heart of central Europe. It covers an area of 83,858sq km and shares borders with eight countries: Switzerland, the Czech Republic, Germany, Liechtenstein, Hungary, Italy, Slovakia and Slovenia. It is one of the most heavily wooded countries in Europe – 46 per cent of the terrain is forested. The Tirol (west) is the most mountainous region – the highest peak is Grossglockner in the eastern Alps (5,019m).

## Winter Sports

• Nearly 50 per cent of the population goes alpine skiing, cross-country skiing or snowboarding regularly.
Austria has:

• 3,500 ski lifts
• 23,000km of groomed pistes
• 500 skiing schools
• 12,400 skiing instructors in 900 resorts
• 1,300 artificial skating rinks
• The first 6-seater chair lift in the world (Doppelmayer)

## The People

• More than 98 per cent of Austria's population of 8,600,000 is German speaking, although there are small minorities of Croats, Hungarians, Slovenes, Czechs, Slovaks and Romany peoples. In a predominantly rural country, Vienna is the only city with a population in excess of one million.

Top: *Viewpoint on the Grossglockner Highway*
Above: *Preparing for ski class in Zell am See*

**Pioneers**
Austria has produced 15 Nobel prize winners, most recently Friedrich von Hayek (Margaret Thatcher's monetarist guru) in 1984. Alfred Nobel was inspired to donate the first peace prize in 1905 after reading the Austrian writer Bertha von Suttner's *Lay Down Your Arms*. Karl Landsteiner, whose portrait appears on the Austrian 1,000 schilling note, won the prize for medicine in 1930 after his discovery of blood groups paved the way for transfusions.

# Essence of Austria

*Many Tirolean farmhouses offer accommodation to visitors*

*Tranquil Sölden makes an excellent base in the Ötztal*

Though no longer the centre of a multinational empire, Austria retains a strong regional diversity. Hungarian influences in the east, Slovenian and Italian in the south, Swiss in the west, and German and Czech in the north mean that, even today, there's not one but many Austrias at the heart of Europe. Vienna apart, the culture is predominantly rural rather than urban, with the emphasis on traditional values and customs. Austria is a deeply conservative country and its people, especially in the Catholic areas, are remarkably devout (ten of the national holidays are religious in origin). As a people, Austrians are invariably friendly and courteous and everywhere you go you'll be assured of a warm welcome.

# THE 10 ESSENTIALS

*If you only have a short time to visit Austria, and would like to sample the very best that the country has to offer, here are the essentials:*

• **Visit a *Heuriger*** These vineyard taverns are for sampling the new wines while listening to folksy music in relaxed garden surroundings.

• **Take a boat trip** Austria is blessed with countless beautiful lakes, Wörther See, Neusiedler See and Hallstätter See, to name but three.

*Morning coffee on the Hallstätter See*

• **Go to a concert** Austria is renowned as a land of music – at least nine famous composers were either born or made their home here.

• **Breathe the mountain air** Whatever the season, head for the mountains – use the networks of cable-cars and chair-lifts.

• **Take a stroll through old Vienna** Admire the stately architecture of the Graben on your way to Stephansdom (St Stephen's Cathedral).

• **Visit a traditional coffee house** Read the morning paper over a coffee and pastry.

• **Pay homage to Mozart** Visit Mozart's birthplace and apartment in Salzburg.

• **Visit a mine** Something of an Austrian speciality, the workings of the salt and silver mines which made the country prosperous are now among its top tourist attractions.

• **Try some regional cooking** Wherever you're staying in Austria, there'll be at least one local dish to savour. There can be few more satisfying ways to learn about a country's traditions.

• **Explore the Wienerwald (Vienna Woods)** One of central Europe's most famous green spaces can be enjoyed on foot, on horseback, in a car or by bike.

*Folk dancer in traditional costume, Kitzbühel*

9

# The Shaping of Austria

**c1,000–500 BC**
Evidence of Iron and Bronze Age peoples working the saltmines of the Salzkammergut and the iron ore deposits around Klagenfurt.

**15 BC**
The Romans reach the Danube which, from now on, will mark the eastern frontier of the Empire. Major Roman settlements in the region include Vindobona (Vienna), Juvavum (Salzburg) and Carnuntum.

**CAD 430**
The Romans retreat from the Danube region.

**976–1246**
Now part of the Holy Roman Empire, Austria is ruled by the Babenberg dynasty.

**1278**
Rudolf of Hapsburg succeeds the Babenbergs and becomes Duke of Austria. His dynasty rules over the country for the next 640 years.

**1477**
Hapsburg power continues to grow as Maximilian I marries Mary of Burgundy.

**1529**
Vienna is besieged by the Turks.

**1556**
Charles V abdicates, dividing his vast empire among members of his family. His brother Ferdinand I receives Austria, Bohemia and Hungary.

**1618–48**
Thirty Years War. The Hapsburgs increasingly identify with Catholic interests.

**1683**
Ottoman Turks defeated at the gates of Vienna.

**1740–65**
Reign of Maria Theresa whose disputed claim to the throne leads to the War of Austrian Succession. Her daughter, Marie-Antoinette, marries the future king Louis XVI of France.

**1765–90**
Reign of Josef II. Edict of Toleration (1781) allows freedom of worship throughout the Empire.

**1805–15**
During the Napoleonic Wars, French troops twice occupy Vienna and Franz II is forced to renounce his title of Holy Roman Emperor.

**1814–15**
Congress of Vienna redraws the map of Europe.

*Empress Maria Theresa, daughter of Charles VI*

**1848**
Revolution breaks out against absolutist Hapsburg rule. Franz-Josef becomes Emperor and reigns until 1916.

**1854–6**
Crimean War. Austria sides with the western powers against Russia.

**1859**
Austria loses Lombardy to the Italian kingdom of Piedmont.

**1866–7**
Following her defeat by Prussia at the Battle of Königgrätz, the Austrian Empire is transformed into the Dual Monarchy of Austria-Hungary.

*Archduke Franz Ferdinand and wife, shortly before his assassination*

**1908**
Annexation of Bosnia-Herzegovina increases ethnic tensions throughout Austria-Hungary.

**1914–18**
Outbreak of World War I – triggered by the assassination of Austrian Archduke Franz-Ferdinand in Sarajevo, Bosnia. Austria allies with Germany. In November 1918 the last emperor, Karl I, abdicates.

**1919**
Karl Renner becomes the first Chancellor of the truncated Austrian Republic.

**1933–4**
Authoritarian regime of Engelbert Dollfuss. In June 1934 Dollfuss is assassinated by the Nazis but their attempted coup fails.

**1938**
Austria is invaded by Nazi Germany and incorporated into the Greater German Reich. The annexation (*Anschluss*) is approved in a referendum.

**1939–45**
World War II. Austria fights with Germany.

**1945**
After Russian troops occupy Vienna, democracy is restored under Allied supervision. Austria is divided into British, French, American and Russian occupied zones and Vienna into sectors.

**1955**
Belvedere Treaty. Allied troops withdraw from Austria which proclaims its neutrality and joins the Council of Europe.

**1986**
During the presidential election the war record of Kurt Waldheim, former Secretary General of the United Nations, becomes an issue. Nevertheless, Waldheim is elected.

**1995**
Austria becomes a full member of the European Union.

**1999**
Austria signs up to the Euro.

11

# Peace & Quiet

*Alpine meadows, as here at Oberau, are a riot of colour in spring and summer*

From the Tirolean Alps to the rolling hills and vineyards of Burgenland, Austria is a land of contrasts with wonderful opportunities for rambling, hiking, birdwatching, picnicking and generally making the most of the peace and quiet.

## Flatlands

Close to the Hungarian border is the vast steppe lake known as the Neusiedler See. The reedbeds and marshes are the habitat of more than 250 species of birds including purple herons, storks, curlews, bitterns, lapwings and golden eagles. It's also home to the suslik (ground squirrel) and to rare butterflies like the steppe winter moth. Camphor weed, feather grass, dwarf iris, helleborines and other rare plants form part of the vegetation. Look out for the messy storks' nests on chimneys in the lakeside villages of Illmitz and Rust – the cartwheels attached to some roofs are there to attract the birds, which are said to bring good luck.

## Mountains

Think of Austria, and alpine images are those likeliest to spring to mind. Just 50km southwest of Vienna, on the

Hohe Wand, chamois balance on the most precarious of rocky ledges, while from spring onwards the meadows are ablaze with wild flowers as flocks of alpine choughs twist and somersault overhead.

Further west, in the Tirolean Alps, cable-cars and skilifts carry you to the mountain peaks for unrivalled vistas across the snowcapped Kitzbüheler, Zillertaler and Stubaier ranges. The Patscherkofel, near Innsbruck, is the land of the pink alpenrose and the delicate white edelweiss – blue gentians also flourish here. Red deer thrive on the coarse grass and if you're lucky you may even catch a glimpse of a snowfinch; the furry marmot on the other hand is likely to prove more elusive.

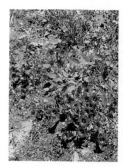

## Forest

Despite its proximity to the capital, the expansive Wienerwald (Vienna Woods) boasts an abundance of wildlife – red squirrels, woodpeckers and fly catchers are all commonplace and you should also be able to spot several species of orchid hidden among the oak, beech and hornbeam. However, in terms of density and sheer variety of foliage, the Wienerwald is trumped by the forests of Steiermark (Styria) and Kärnten (Carinthia) with their richer textures and darker tones. Here, musty odours of mushroom and moss mingle with the sweet scent of pine, spruce and larch.

*Look out for the intense blue of low-growing gentians above the tree line*

*A purple heron – one of 250 bird species found around Neusiedler See*

## National Parks

There are six National Parks in Austria, with plans for a seventh on the German border.

**Nationalpark Hohe Tauern** (► 19): a vast alpine nature reserve of 1,787sq km, in three provinces (eastern Tirol, Carinthia and Salzburg).

**Nationalpark Neusiedler See-Seewinkel:** the only steppe reserve in central Europe, best visited in spring and autumn when the migrating birds arrive.

**Nationalpark Nockberge:** a region of traditional farmland, lying between the Lieser Valley and the Turracher Höhe Range in Carinthia, at an altitude of 1,300–2,440m.

**Nationalpark Donau-Auen:** the largest single wetland in central Europe, home to more than 5,000 animal species.

**Nationalpark Thayatla:** meadowland on the border with the Czech Republic.

**Nationalpark Kalkalpen:** covering 21,000ha in the Pyhrn-Eisenwurzen region, is a typical high-alpine park.

# Austria's Famous

## Wolfgang Amadeus Mozart

A child prodigy, born in Salzburg in 1756, Mozart spent much of his childhood travelling through Europe. He became Concertmaster to the Archbishop of Salzburg in 1771, but after a frustrating 10 years moved to Vienna. When Mozart presented Joseph II with the score of one of his operas in 1782 the Emperor is supposed to have remarked: 'Too beautiful for our ears, dear Mozart, and an awful lot of notes'.

During his ten years in Vienna Mozart wrote more than 240 compositions, from operas, symphonies and concertos to pieces for glass harmonica and clockwork organ. His professional career was dogged by imperial stinginess, bad luck, poor judgement and the petty spite of colleagues – Antonio Salieri orchestrated the intrigues at court. At the time of his death in December 1791 Mozart was facing financial ruin but had he lived only six months longer, he would almost certainly have been appointed to the post he had always coveted, that of *Kappelmeister* (Master of Music) at St Stephen's Cathedral, Vienna.

## Sigmund Freud

Born in Moravia in 1856, Freud moved to Vienna when he was three. After studying medicine, he became interested in hypnotherapy and the role played by dreams in the subconscious (a plaque on Himmelstrasse marks the spot where the idea first occurred to him).

Freud lived the life of a typical Viennese citizen, taking a daily constitutional along Ringstrasse, playing cards in the Café Landtmann and enjoying holidays in the Salzkammergut. By the 1920s he had become a household name. His discovery (which is now disputed) that infantile sexual impulses lay at the root of most adult neuroses caused a sensation. Freud fled Austria in 1938 to escape Nazi persecution. He died in London the following year.

**Arnold Schwarzenegger**
Born in 1947 in Thal, a village near Graz, Schwarzenegger began life as a body-builder, winning five Mr Universe titles before embarking on a film career after settling in the USA. His unpronounceable name and heavy accent were obvious drawbacks, but in 1984 'Arnie' finally struck gold with *Terminator* and is now one of the industry's highest earners.

Above: *Arnold Schwarzenegger shows no sign of slowing down in his fifties* Right: *the father of psychoanalysis, Sigmund Freud*

# Top Ten

Above: *The Kunsthistorisches Museum, Vienna*
Right: *Golden eagles can sometimes be seen in the Rauristal valley*

# 1
# Dürnstein

46B4

70km west of Vienna

Dürnstein

Rathaus ☎ 0271 12 19

Stiftskirche: Apr–Oct, Mon–Sat 9–6, Sun 10–6

Few

Melk (➤ 23), Krems an der Donau (➤ 55), Mariazell (➤ 57)

*With its romantic castle ruins and breathtaking Danube views, the little walled town of Dürnstein is the most photogenic spot in the Wachau region.*

The village itself is tiny but picturesque. The 16th-century houses on Hauptstrasse with Renaissance balconies and oriel windows are especially appealing. Don't miss the Stiftskirche, the former Augustinian monastery, with its exquisite blue-and-white baroque tower, erected in 1725.

It's a 15–30 minute climb from the Steiner Tor (Stone Gateway) to the ruined fortress where King Richard the Lionheart of England was held captive by Leopold, Duke of Austria in 1193 – the two had fallen out during the Third Crusade. According to legend, Richard's minstrel, Blondel, set out to find his master and, on reaching the castle at Dürnstein, began to sing one of the king's favourite melodies. Richard recognised the tune and took up the refrain but, despite Blondel's efforts, continued to languish in jail for more than a year. He was finally released after the payment of a huge ransom. The castle was dismantled by the Swedes during the Thirty Years War but there are outstanding views of the river valley from the ruins.

After sampling the famous local wine, *Grüner Veltliner*, you could explore other beauty spots in the region: Weissenkirchen (another wine-producing village), the Kuernringer castle ruins at Aggstein, the pilgrimage churches of Maria Langegg and Maria Taferl, and of course Melk Abbey (➤ 23).

*The baroque tower of the Stiftskirche is a prominent landmark in the Danube valley*

# 2
# Eisriesenwelt

*The 'World of the Ice Giants' is how the Austrians describe this extraordinary natural phenomenon – one of the largest ice cave networks on earth.*

✚ 64A3

✉ Abtenau, near Werfen, 30km south of Salzburg

☎ 06628 42690

🕐 Tours May, Jun, Sep 9:30–3:30 hourly; Jul–Aug 9:30–4:30 hourly

🍴 Restaurant (££)

🚌 Eisriesenwelt-Linie, May–Oct approx two-hourly (more frequently if demand); cable-car May, Jun, Sep–early Oct 9–5; Jul–Aug 9–6

♿ Not accessible

✋ Expensive (all inclusive ticket available)

↔ Salzburg (➤ 66)

*The ice caves at Eisriesenwelt are enhanced by skilful lighting*

Allow at least half a day for a visit to these shining ice caves. Before starting out you'll need a stout pair of shoes, a sweater and a pair of gloves – forget how warm it is on the outside, the temperature inside the caves hovers at around zero degrees centigrade.

The route from Werfen allows for spectacular views of the surrounding countryside. The 5km-long mountain road climbs to the car park, from where it's a 15- minute walk to the cable-car. The footpath overlooks the Salzach Valley and the majestic Hohenwerfen Fortress. From the cable-car it's another 15–20 minute walk to the main entrance of the caves themselves, 1,640m above the valley floor.

The guided tour lasts about 75 minutes. Visitors climb the steps to the gallery where the real show begins. The frozen waterfalls, glaciers, stalactites and ice curtains are lit to brilliant effect, giving the walls a bluish-white sheen. Altogether the caves extend more than 42km from the western cliff of the Hochkogel – the walls are more than 20m thick in places. Some of the more spectacular forma-tions have fanciful names like 'Palace of the Ice Giants', 'Ice Queen's Veil' and 'The Cathedral'.

Werfen itself has a wonderful mountain setting and you may be tempted to stay the night. If so, don't fail to sign up for the guided tour of the Hohenwerfen Fortress to see the Knights Hall, the torture chamber, the chapel with its fresco of the apocalypse, and the birds of prey that circle dramatically overhead.

# 3
# Hallstatt

✚ 64B3

✉ 50km southeast of Salzburg

🚆 Hallstatt, then ferry

🚢 Schiffahrt Hemetsberger
☎ 06134 8228 (ferry from train and lake trips)

ℹ️ Seestrasse 169
☎ 06134 8208

↔️ Bad Ischl (► 71), Gmunden (► 72)

❓ Corpus Christi lake festival (► 116)

**Salzbergwerk (salt mines)**

☎ 06134 8251-72

🕐 May, mid–Sep to late Oct 9:30–3:30; June–mid Sep 9:30–4:30

🍴 Restaurant (££) (► 96)

♿ Physically handicapped and children under 4 excluded from mines for safety reasons

✋ Expensive

❓ Guided tours (allow 2hrs)

*There scarcely seems to be space for Hallstatt between lake and mountain*

*Described in the 19th century as 'the loveliest lakeside village in the world', Hallstatt lies at the heart of the scenic Salzkammergut 'lake district'.*

The word *Salz* means 'salt' and it was this commodity that made Hallstatt a thriving commercial centre before Rome was even thought of. The prehistoric finds, including bronze dishes from the Danube, amber from northern Germany, glass from Italy and ivory from Africa, were considered so important that the era from 800–400 BC is now universally known as the 'Hallstatt Period'.

The village is wedged between the Hallstätter See and the Dachstein Mountains – there's no room for a railway line, so you have to travel across the lake by boat. Hallstatt's 16th-century parish church (Pfarrkirche), is the focal point of an annual Corpus Christi procession at the end of May. Note the colourful frescoes over the porch and don't miss the gorgeous winged altarpiece on the Gothic high altar. The charnel house next door is a no-holds-barred *memento mori*, with row upon row of neatly arranged skulls and bones, many of them painted and inscribed with names and dates.

A funicular will take you 350m above the village to the oldest working **salt mines** in the world, first exploited in the Neolithic era. The guided tour is an absolute must. Visitors don protective clothing, then board the mine train which trundles 2km into the Christina tunnel. You see a film on the history of the mine, slide down a wooden chute to an underground lake, look down on an illuminated crater and walk the final 185m to the train and daylight. You can then finish off with a meal in the Rudolfsturm, a medieval tower built in 1284 to protect the mine.

# 4
# Hohe Tauern

*The largest national park in central Europe, with an area of nearly 1,800sq km, Hohe Tauern is a beautiful and unspoilt natural landscape.*

81E2

60km south of Salzburg

04875 51261–0

All year

Restaurants (££–£££)

Zell am See, Lienz, Badgastein

Zell am See (➤ 89); Badgastein Kaiser-Franz-Josef-Strasse 06434 2531; Lienz Europlatz 1 04852 6526-5; Matrei Hauptplatz 04875 6257

Free entry to park

Zell am See (➤ 89), Kitzbühel (➤ 20)

*The three mighty waterfalls at Krimml, just to the north of the Hohe Tauern, fall a total of 380m*

The park is administered jointly by the Salzburger Land, Kärnten (Carinthia) and Tirol. If you're intending to explore the park for any length of time, Zell am See (➤ 89), Lienz, Bad Gastein and Matrei make attractive and convenient bases. The tourist offices can provide you with information about free parking, taxi shuttles, visitors centres, overnight refuges and the all-important route maps. The park authorities have come up with more than 80 tour suggestions – each includes a summary of what you're likely to see, as well as information about parking, access and walking times. Besides walking and hiking, activities catered for include rock climbing, kayaking, alpine rafting and fishing.

The hiking trails (all clearly marked and signposted) include a number of specially designated 'family routes' which explain the particular natural environment and the underpinning ecosystem. One of the more unusual is the Römerstrasse, a pack trail forged by Roman soldiers 2,000 years ago to secure the trade in wine and salt.

Wherever you go the scenery ranges from the stunning to the spectacular: gorges and ravines, waterfalls and mountain lakes, alpine meadows ablaze with wild flowers, virgin forests of larch and stone pine. On your travels you may encounter alpine salamanders, golden and sea eagles, vultures, marmots, red deer, ibex and the elusive chamois.

Cars are excluded from Hohe Tauern, with the single exception of the famous Grossglockner Highway (➤ 88). The other star attraction is the Krimml Falls, easily accessed from Zell am See.

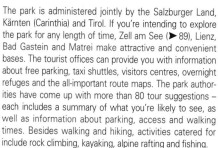

# 5

# Kitzbühel

*Kitzbühel in winter –
charming if expensive*

*One of Austria's oldest and most glamorous
ski resorts, Kitzbühel also offers wonderful
opportunities for walking and cycling in summer.*

✚ 81E3

✉ 80km east of Innsbruck

ℹ Hinterstadt 18
☎ 05356 62155-0

🚆 Kitzbühel

🚌 Bus to ski fields; cable-
car services to the
peaks via the Bergbahn

↔ Hohe Tauern (► 19),
Zell am See (► 89)

❓ World cup skiing Jan;
Tirolean evenings
(Eurotours ☎ 05356
71304); open-air
concerts (Jul, Aug)

**Cable Car Museum**

✉ Hahnenkamm Mountain
Station

🕐 Daily 10–6

Kitzbühel's prosperity initially derived from silver and
copper mining. It was only at the end of the 19th century
with the arrival of the first party of Norwegian skiers that
the town discovered an even more lucrative source of
income. The wooded valley provides an attractive
backdrop to the local sights – a couple of historic churches,
as well as several rows of handsome 16th- and 17th-
century burgher's houses, all brightly painted. Prices are
steep during the skiing season, especially in the glitziest
bars and discos, but the increasing number of package
tourists has introduced a welcome note of realism.

Most skiers head for the Kitzbüheler Horn (1,996m) and
the Hahnenkamm (1,600m). There are more than 60 runs,
mainly suited to beginners and intermediates although
there are a handful of black runs on the Hahnenkamm.
Other winter sports available include cross-country skiing,
snowboarding and tobogganing.

A major attraction in the summer is the Alpine Flower
Garden on the Kitzbüheler Horn, a riot of colour with 120
different species. The tourist office provides maps and
leaflets detailing cycle routes and more than forty walks
through the lush alpine meadows. You can also take a ride
up the Hahnenkamm to visit the **Cable-Car Museum**.

# 6
# Kunsthistorisches Museum, Vienna

*This fabulous art collection, one of the most important in the world, was moved from the Belvedere to its present premises in 1891.*

Brueghel the Elder's Peasant Wedding *(1568)*

Designed by Gottfried Semper and Karl Hasenauer, the Kunsthistorisches Museum is something of a work of art itself. On the ground floor you'll find the Oriental and Egyptian collections, Greek and Roman antiquities, sculpture and decorative arts. As there are more than 4km of galleries, you'll need to be selective – pick up a copy of the museum plan before you set out.

The picture gallery is on the first floor and the collection reflects Hapsburg tastes and the territories over which they ruled. The Netherlands are especially well represented – there are more paintings by Pieter Brueghel the Elder here than anywhere else in the world. They include the masterpieces, *Hunters in the Snow*, *Peasant Wedding*, *Children's Games* and the satirical *Battle between Carnival and Lent*. Other highlights among the Dutch and Flemish Old Masters are a *Crucifixion* triptych by Rogier van der Weyden, several portraits by Rembrandt (including one of his mother) and an entire room of Van Dycks. The scale and ambition of Rubens' altarpieces will take your breath away. Many of the Italian paintings were acquired in the 17th century by Archduke Leopold Wilhelm. Rome is represented by Raphael, Venice by Bellini, Tintoretto and Titian – only the Prado has more paintings by this artist.

✚ 34B2

✉ Maria-Theresien-Platz/Burgring 5

☎ 01521 770

🕐 Tue–Wed, Fri–Sun 10–6; Thu 10–9

🍴 Café on first floor (££)

🚇 Babenberger Strasse, Volkstheater

🚌 1, 2

♿ Good (elevator entrance at Burgring 5)

✋ Moderate

🔄 Hofburg (➤ 32), Sezession (➤ 42), Spanische Reitschule (➤ 44)

❓ Frequent lectures and exhibitions

21

# 7

# Maria Wörth and Wörther See

 64B1

📧 100km west of Graz

🚂 Klagenfurt, Pörtschach, Velden

🚢 Wörther See Schiffahrt, Klagenfurt, ☎ 0463 21155, round trip to Velden 3hr 45min

ℹ Klagenfurt (▶ 75); Portschäch
📧 Hauptstrasse 153, ☎ 04272 2354;
Velden 📧 Seecorso 2, ☎ 04272 4488

**Pyramidenkogel**

🕐 Daily Apr, Oct 10–6; May, Sep 9–7; Jun 9–8; Jul, Aug 9–10

♿ Few

**Wildpark Rosegg**

📧 5km south of Velden

🕐 9–5 (Jul, Aug till 6)

✋ Moderate

*Maria Wörth's parish church is surrounded on three sides by water*

*The composer Gustav Mahler was inspired to write some of his greatest music while vacationing on the shores of this beautiful inland lake.*

Mahler was especially taken with Maria Wörth and its idyllic setting on a peninsula reaching out into the lake. His villa lies hidden among the woods at Maiernigg, near Klagenfurt (▶ 75) – the cabin where he worked each summer is open to visitors. The Karawanken Alps stretch into the distance, while the two pilgrimage churches here are 'must sees' for their medieval frescoes and statuary. Boat excursions leave from Klagenfurt for Maria Wörth and several other destinations along the lake. For romantics there are moonlight cruises on board the *Thalia*, a restored passenger steamer dating from 1908.

The promenade at Pörtschach is perfect for an evening stroll after a day spent on the beach (you can swim as early as May here) while the nightlife rivals that of Velden, the busiest of the resorts. Windsurfing, sailing and water skiing are all possible in Velden but if the crowds begin to pall, leave the boutiques and café terraces behind for **Wildpark Rosegg**, a wildlife park with white wolves, lynx, bison and birds of prey.

Finding somewhere to stay isn't a problem. If money is no object, consider one of the converted lakeside villas built around the turn of the century for the Viennese business elite. More economical alternatives include Krumpendorf, a spa near Velden, or Reifnitz, a quiet little town only a few kilometres drive from the 850m-high **Pyramidenkogel** (observation tower) with unbeatable views of the Carinthian countryside, weather permitting.

# 8
# Melk

*Melk has been an important spiritual and cultural centre for more than 1,000 years. The town is famous for its Benedictine abbey, founded in 1089.*

Left: *Melk Abbey has a commanding position above the Danube*

Melk Abbey, a spectacular masterpiece of baroque architecture, is perched on a rocky promontory high above the Danube. It was renowned as a medieval seat of learning and inspired Umberto Eco's detective novel *The Romance of the Rose* (Melk too was destroyed by fire, on more than one occasion).

Highlights of the guided tour include the abbey church, completed in 1736 by Jakob Prandtauer, the library, the Marble Hall and the superb Kaiserstiege (Imperial Staircase) which paves the way for the 190m-long gallery known as the Kaisergang. The church's sumptuous, almost theatrical interior with its gilded stucco embelish-ments, Italianate paintings by Johann Michael Rottmayr, carved pulpit and magnificent dome takes the breath away. The monastic library contains more than 80,000 books as well as precious illuminated manuscripts dating back to the 12th century. The ceiling fresco by Paul Troger is a masterpiece. The Marble Hall (Marmorsaal) is also impressive, no less so when you realise that the columns are *faux-marbre* and not the genuine article. Among the guests to have been entertained here are Empress Maria Theresa, Pope Pius VI and Napoleon. The views of the town and the river from the terrace are breathtaking.

The town, some 50m below the monastery, has some quaint houses including the former monastery tavern, a beautifully preserved Renaissance post office, fortified towers and a 15th-century parish church with an unusual calvary.

Above: *The Abbey's magnificent library*

✚ 46B3

✉ 85km west of Vienna

ℹ Babenbergerstrasse 1
☎ 02752 2307-32

🚆 Emmersdorf an der Donau (3 km)

↔ Krems an der Donau (► 55), Dürnstein (► 16)

❓ Melk Summer Festival (theatre); baroque music at Whitsun

**Melk Abbey**

✉ Abt Berthold Dietmayr-Strasse 1 ☎ 02752 2312

🕐 Apr–Oct, daily 9–5

🍴 Restaurant (££)

♿ None

👆 Moderate

23

# 9
## Schloss Schönbrunn, Vienna

✚ 34B1

✉ Schönbrunner Schlossstrasse 47

☎ 01 81113

🕐 Palace: 1 Apr–30 Oct 8:30–5; 31 Oct–31 Mar 8:30–4:30; Coach Museum 9–6:30; zoo: summer 9–6:30, winter 9–sunset; park: 6–sunset

🍴 Café and Tirolean restaurant (££)

Ⓢ Schönbrunn, Hietzing

🚌 15A, 10, 58

♿ Good (full disabled access – contact information desk)

✋ Expensive

❓ Imperial Tour 22 rooms (35 mins); Grand Tour 40 rooms (50 mins). Free. Audio-guide available

*This palatial summer residence, built for Maria Theresa in 1743–9, is actually a scaled-down version of an earlier, more ambitious design.*

Schönbrunn takes its name from the 'beautiful spring' discovered here by Emperor Matthias in the 17th century. Fischer von Erlach's extravagant plans for the palace, intended to rival Versailles, were abandoned when Maria Theresa called for a summer residence that would serve as a family home for her consort and their 16 children. Even so, there are 1,441 rooms!

The 'Grand Tour' comprises the apartments of Emperor Franz-Josef and Empress Elizabeth, the ceremonial and state halls and the audience chambers of Maria Theresa – 40 rooms in all. The interiors are an artistic treasure house – frescoes, trompe l'oeil paintings, marquetry, lacquer work, stucco, gilded mirrors, Gobelin tapestries, marble and crystal. No expense was spared: the 'Room of Millions' alone cost one million guilders – a huge sum when a court servant's wages were 30 guilders a year. The most impressive of Schönbrunn's reception rooms is the aptly named Large Gallery – 43m long and 10m high. Since 1761 it has been used for innumerable state occasions, including the Congress of Vienna in 1814–15 and the Vienna Summit in 1961 between US President John F Kennedy and Soviet leader, Nikita Khrushchev.

Yet for all the pomp and circumstance of court ceremony many of the rooms were actually lived in, and

herein lies the real interest. The round Chinese Room, for example, has a dumb waiter for intimate private dinners and a secret staircase used by Maria Theresa for assignations with her lover, the Austrian chancellor. You can also see the Hall of Mirrors where the Empress took the six-year old Mozart onto her lap, and the room belonging to the most famous of her daughters, Marie Antoinette. Franz-Josef's apartments are in another part of the building. From behind his desk in the Writing Room the sad-eyed Emperor with the distinctive mutton-chop whiskers, who liked to refer to himself as the nation's 'highest ranking civil servant', doggedly administered the affairs of state for 68 years. His spartan tastes are evident in his private bedroom, although he did allow himself one or two luxuries – an en suite ashtray and reading shelf in the adjoining toilet for example. The tastes of his beautiful wife Elizabeth (Sisi) were far more luxurious – witness her state-of-the-art bathroom with marble bath, shower and hair hook to protect her long tresses from the water. One senses the extent to which the two led separate but equally isolated lives.

*Schönbrunn's immense façade (bottom) prepares you for the sumptuous apartments within (below)*

After the tour, spend some time in the immaculate formal gardens and landscaped park. There are magnificent views of Vienna from the triumphal gate known as the Gloriette. There's also the world's oldest surviving zoo, a Butterfly House and a Carriage Museum with more than 100 ceremonial coaches, sedan chairs and prams, dating back to 1690. If you leave via the Hietzing exit you'll see the Emperor's private railway station.

# 10
# Stephansdom, Vienna

*The bright patterns on Stephansdom's roof are created with glazed tiles*

*In this city with few high-rise buildings, St Stephen's Cathedral, with its chevroned roof and soaring Gothic tower, is a distinctive landmark.*

✠ 35D3

✉ Stephansplatz 3

☎ 01 515 52526

🕐 Daily 6AM–10PM. Guided tours Mon–Sat 10:30, 3 (Jul–Aug also 7); Sun 3. Restricted access during services

🚇 Stephansplatz

🚌 1A

♿ Good

💵 Cathedral: free. Tour of choir: moderate

↔ Kapuzinergruft (► 33), Museum für Angewandte Kunst (► 36), Obizzi-Palais (► 33), Peterskirche (► 36)

❓ Separate tours of catacombs

The cathedral was consecrated in 1147 but only the Riesentor (Giant's Door) and the flanking 'pagan towers' are left over from the various Romanesque churches. Work on the present building began early in the 14th century. The south tower, known as 'Steffl' (Little Steve), dates from 1359 and is 137m high if you include the double-headed eagle. You can climb the 343 steps for views, or take the lift up the north tower to see the great bell Pommerin, or 'Boomer', cast from abandoned Turkish cannon in 1683.

Don't miss the carved stone pulpit by Anton Pilgram (1510), a masterpiece of filigree work featuring highly individualised portraits of the Church Fathers and of the sculptor himself (seen peering from a window). Worshippers light votive candles to the miraculous Pötscher Madonna, said to have saved the city from the Turks in 1697 after shedding human tears. While you can just about see the superb Gothic vaulting of the choir from the nave, you'll get closer on the guided tour. The sublime Wiener Neustädter altar of 1447 is one of the highlights. You'll also be shown the stone effigies of Rudolph IV and his consort, Catherine of Bohemia, and the exquisite red marble tomb of Frederick III (1470). The lid alone weighs 8,700kg and the sculptor, Niclaus von Leyden, somehow managed to squeeze in more than 240 figures, as well as 32 coats of arms.

# What To See

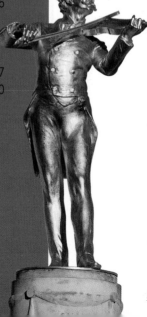

Above: Kaffee und Kuchen, *an Austrian tradition*
Right: *The Johann Strauss statue in Vienna's Stadtpark*

27

(D) Germany    (CH) Switzerland

(FL) Liechtenstein    (I) Italy

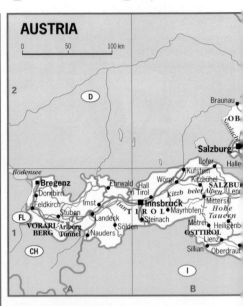

**AUSTRIA**

0    50    100 km

*In Linz there are baroque splendours round every street corner*

CZ Czech Republic       H Hungary

SK Slovakia            SLO Slovenia

*Mozart is honoured in Vienna's Burggarten*

*Fiacre rides are a reminder of Vienna's imperial past*

# Wien (Vienna)

Whatever the truth of Mozart senior's perception (see below), music and dancing have always been an integral part of the Viennese way of life. It's no accident that the waltz, queen of ballroom dances, originated in this most elegant and stylish of cities and hardly surprising that the Strausses, father and son, are as popular now as they were in their 19th-century heyday. A quintessentially Viennese phenomenon, Strauss mania manifests itself in a seamless succession of concerts, exhibitions, film festivals and of course the *Fasching* (carnival) balls for which Vienna is famous. The *joie de vivre* is infectious and, if you find it just a little over the top, consider Johann Strauss the Younger, or Wild Johnny as he was known in the family – one of the greatest showmen of the age. On one occasion in 1872 he serenaded an audience of 100,000 Americans with an orchestra of no fewer than 1,000 musicians!

> *'The Viennese dislike and misunderstand everything serious and sensible; they care only for burlesques, harlequinades, magical tricks, farces and antics.'*
>
> LEOPOLD MOZART
> writing to his son (1781)

●

# The City

Exuberance has always been one aspect of the Viennese character but the citizens of this great capital have not always had reason to celebrate. In the aftermath of World War II Vienna was one vast bomb site, as depicted in the film *The Third Man*. This was the city of shabby intriguers, spies and foreign troops – like Berlin, the city was divided into four occupied sectors. Today it's very much a part of a Europe united rather than divided. Not that Vienna is ashamed of its past – far from it. The marks of the imperial capital of the Hapsburgs are evident everywhere: in the elegant Historicist architecture of the Ring, in the genteel and sophisticated cafés, in the museums, concert halls and palaces. And, while it's true that Vienna is now the capital of a very reduced and homogeneous population compared with its polyglot past, it still has the cosmopolitan hallmarks of a world city.

Exploring Vienna is not only a joy, it couldn't be easier. One reason is its size. Despite having a population of 1.5 million, Vienna is surprisingly compact and perfect for strolling. There are a number of pedestrianised areas and most of the traffic is carried by the Ring, the stately boulevard that girdles the inner city. If you do become tired, you can resort to the fast and efficient metro system or to the distinctive red and white trams that rumble about town, offering visitors a cheap and entertaining sightseeing tour.

*The sparkling interior of the Josefstadt Theatre*

*A Lippizaner stallion is put through his paces at the Spanish Riding School*

✚ 34C3
✉ Josefsplatz 1
☎ 534 10297
🕐 State Apartments: 9–5;
  Treasury: Fri–Wed, 10–6,
  Thu 10–9; Burgkapelle:
  Tue–Thu 1:30–3:30, Fri
  1–3
🚇 Herrengasse
🚌 Hopper 3A
♿ Few
💲 Expensive
↔ Kapuzinergruft (➤ 33),
  Spanische Reitschule
  (➤ 44)

*The Hofburg's grand
entrance on
Michaelerplatz*

## HOFBURG (IMPERIAL PALACE)　　★★★

The history of the Hofburg begins in the 13th century with the building of a fortress by Rudolph I, founder of the Hapsburg dynasty. However, it was not until 1619 that the palace finally became the official residence of the court. A city within a city, the vast complex of royal apartments and administrative buildings covers an area of 240,000sq m. There are 2,600 rooms, 19 courtyards, 18 wings and 54 main staircases. More than 5,000 people still live or work here, including the Austrian president and his officials.

The imperial apartments are open to visitors, mostly the 19th-century rooms belonging to Emperor Franz-Josef and Empress Elizabeth. Her dressing room contains some of her exercise equipment but there are few other human touches and the summer apartments at Schönbrunn are more evocative (➤ 24–5). The oldest building in the Hofburg is the 15th-century Burgkapelle (court chapel), where the Vienna Boys' Choir sings mass on Sunday mornings (sadly, tickets are like gold dust – ➤ 112). This is where royal marriages took place and the hearts of the Hapsburgs are contained in urns in the crypt. More impressive is the white marble tomb of Archduchess Maria Christina, a masterpiece by the Italian sculptor, Antonio Canova. Royal regalia, including the 10th-century crown of Emperor Otto the Great, are on display in the Schatzkammer (Treasury). The Hofburg is best seen from

Michaelerplatz – the beautifully proportioned green cupola was incorporated into Fischer von Erlach's design in the 19th century.

Left: *Hofbibliothek interior*
Above: *Time never stands still at the Clock Museum*

## KAPUZINERGRUFT ●●

It was in 1618 that Empress Anna invited the Capuchin Order to found a monastery which would serve as her last resting place. Since then a total of 146 Hapsburgs, including 12 emperors and 17 empresses have been buried in the network of crypts and underground vaults. Many of the bronze sarcophagi are adorned with chilling *memento mori* – skeletal knights in armour, cherubs sounding the last trumpet call, cowering figures, discarded crowns and banners. The most obvious contrast is between the monumental sarcophagus, designed for Maria Theresa and her husband, Franz Stefan, and the plain tomb commissioned by their son, Josef II, who detested ostentation. In 1989 Empress Zita, wife of the last Hapsburg emperor, Karl I, was laid to rest in the crypt.

## KUNSTHISTORISCHES MUSEUM (➤ 21, TOP TEN)

## OBIZZI-PALAIS (CLOCK MUSEUM) ●

In the 17th century this elegant little palace belonged to Ferdinand Obizzi, commander of the Vienna militia. It is now the home of one of the capital's more extraordinary museums: a collection of more than 3,000 timepieces. It reflects not only the history of chronometry from the 15th century, but the artfulness and variety of these useful, if occasionally maddening, devices: water clocks, electric clocks, computerised clocks, astronomical clocks, clocks shaped like rowing boats, grandfather clocks, musical clocks, painted clocks and gilded clocks. Come at 12 noon and you won't be able to hear yourself think for the din!

✚ 34C3
✉ Tegethoffstrasse 2
☎ 512 6853
🕐 Daily 9:30–4
🚇 Stephansplatz
🚌 Hopper 3A
♿ None
✋ Moderate
↔ Hofburg (➤ 32),
Stephansdom (➤ 26)

✚ 34C4
✉ Schulhof 2
☎ 533 2265
🕐 Tue–Sun 9–4:30
🚇 Stephansplatz
🚌 Hopper 2A
♿ None
✋ Moderate (free Fri am except holidays)
↔ Peterskirche (➤ 36),
Stephansdom (➤ 26)

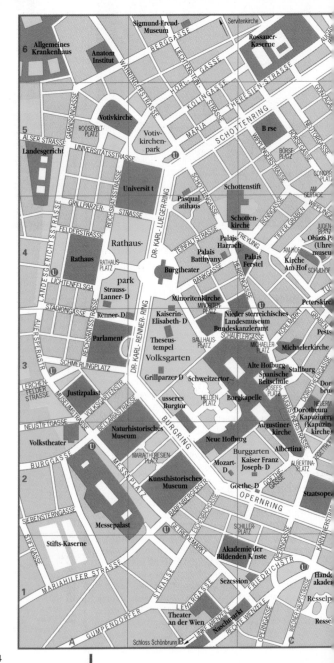

Sigmund-Freud-Museum

Servitenkirche

Allgemeines Krankenhaus

Anatom Institut

Rossauer-Kaserne

6

BERGGASSE

LIECHTENSTEIN GASSE

WÄHRINGERSTRASSE

HÖRL GASSE

KOLINGASSE

GARNISONGASSE

MARIA THERESIEN STRASSE

Votivkirche

Votiv-kirchen-park

ROOSEVELT-PLATZ

5

ALSER STRASSE

Landesgericht

UNIVERSITÄTSSTRASSE

MARIA STRASSE

SCHOTTENRING

B rse

BÖRSE-PLATZ

WIPPLINGERSTRASSE

CONCOR-PLATZ

AM GESTADE

Universit t

Pasqual atihaus

SCHOTTENGASSE

Schottenstift

SCHOTTENGASSE

RENNGASSE

TIEFER GRABEN

WIPPLIN

GRILLPARZER STRASSE

REICHSRATSSTRASSE

TEINFALTSTRASSE

Schotten-kirche

FREYUNG

AM HOF

JUDEN-PLATZ

Rathaus-

Palais Harrach

Palais Batthyany

Palais Ferstel

Obizzi P. (Uhre museu

FELDERSTRASSE

DR. KARL-LUEGER-RING

Kirche Am Hof

SCHUCHOF

4

Rathaus

RATHAUS-PLATZ

park

Burgtheater

BANKGASSE

HERRENGASSE

Peterskirc

LANDESGERICHTSSTRASSE

LICHTENFELSGA

Strauss-Lanner- D

Minoritenkirche

MINORITEN-PLATZ

Niederösterreichisches Landesmuseum

KOHLMARKT

GRÜN

STADIONGASSE

Renner- D

Bundeskanzleramt

SCHAUFLERGASSE

Pests

AUERSPERGSTR.

Parlament

Kaiserin-Elisabeth- D

Theseus-tempel

MICHAELER-PLATZ

Michaelerkirche

3

SCHMERLINGPLATZ

DR. KARL-RENNER-RING

Volksgarten

BALLHAUS-PLATZ

Alte Hofburg

Stallburg

LERCHEN FELDER STRASSE

Justizpalast

Grillparzer D

Schweitzertor

Spanische Reitsche

JOSEFS-PLATZ

Dor bru

MUSEUMSTRASSE

VOLKSGARTENSTR.

usseres Burgtor

HELDEN-PLATZ

Burgkapelle

NEUE BURG

Dorotheum Kapuziner/ (Kapuzin kirche

NEUSTIFTGASSE

BELLARIASTRASSE

Naturhistorisches Museum

BURGRING

Augustiner-kirche

Volkstheater

Neue Hofburg

Albertina

BURGGASSE

MARIATHERESIEN-PLATZ

Burggarten

ALBERTINA-PLATZ

2

MESSEPLATZ

Kunsthistorisches Museum

Mozart- D

Kaiser Franz Joseph- D

GOETHE GASSE

Goethe- D

Staatsope

SIEBENSTERNGASSE

BABENBERGERSTR

OPERNRING

STIFTGASSE

Messepalast

GETREIDEMARKT

SCHILLER-PLATZ

KÄRNTNERS

Stifts-Kaserne

Akademie der Bildenden K nste

FRIEDRICHSTR

1

MARIAHILFER STRASSE

STRASSE

LEHARGASSE

Sezession

Hando akade

Resselp

Theater an der Wien

LINKE WIENZEILE

Naschmarkt

RECHTE WIENZEILE

OPERNGASSE

WIENZEILE

Resse

GUMPENDORFER

Schloss Schönbrunn

A

B

C

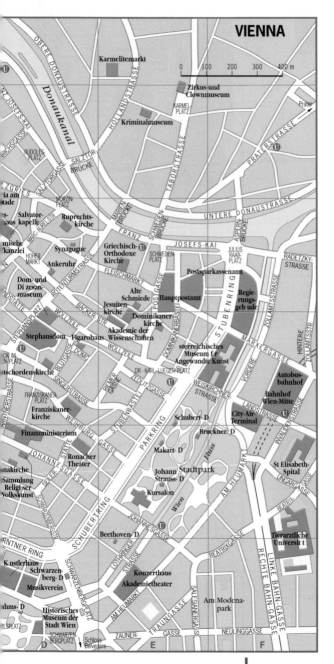

# VIENNA

Karmelitermarkt

0    100    200    300    400 m

Zirkus-und
Clownmuseum

KARMEL-
PLATZ

Prater

Kriminalmuseum

OBERE DONAUSTRASSE

Donaukanal

HOLLANDSTRASSE

TABORSTRASSE

PRATERSTRASSE

NZ-JOSEFS-KAI

RICHSGASSE

RUDOLFS-
PLATZ

SALZTOR-
BRÜCKE

SALZTORGASSE

JULIUS
RAAB-
PLATZ

UNTERE DONAUSTRASSE

ASPERN
BRÜCKE

RADETZKY-
STRASSE

ZGRIES
ia am
cade

MORZIN-
PLATZ

MARIEN-
BRÜCKE

MARC-AUREL-STR

s-
haus

Salvator-
kapelle

Ruprechts-
kirche

FRANZ

SCHWEDEN-
BRÜCKE

JOSEFS-KAI

mische
kanzlei

Synagogue

Griechisch-
Orthodoxe
Kirche

SCHWEDEN-
PLATZ

ZOLLAMTSTRASSE

HOHER
MARKT

Ankeruhr

FLEISCHMARKT

Postsparkassenamt

Dom- und
Di zesan-
museum

ROTENTURMSTRASSE

Alte
Schmiede

Hauptpostamt

STUBENRING

Regie-
rungs-
geb ude

MARXERGASSE

POSTGASSE

NDSTATTE

Jesuiten-
kirche

BACKER-STR

HINTERE
ZOLLAMTSSTR

Stephansplatz

WOLLZEILE

Dominikaner-
kirche

Stephansdom

Figarohaus

Akademie der
Wissenschaften

DOMINIKANERBASTEI

D-DOMG

WOLLZEILE

sterreichisches
Museum f r
Angewandte Kunst

CK IM
N-PLATZ

BLUTGASSE

VORDERE

tschordenskirche

DR.-KARL-LUEGER-PLATZ

Autobus-
bahnhof

SINGERSTRASSE

RIEMER
GASSE

 SCHULERSTRASSE

FRANZISKANER-
PLATZ

TEGLTZGASSE

WEISKIRCHNER-
STRASSE

Bahnhof
Wien-Mitte

LANDSTRASSE

INVALIDENSTRASSE

Franziskaner-
kirche

STUBENBASTEI

City-Air
Terminal

WEIHBURG-
GASSE

Finanzministerium

PARKRING

Schubert- D

St Elisabeth-
Spital

SEILERSTATTE

JOHANNESGASSE

Ronacher
Theater

Bruckner- D

AM HEUMARKT

UNGARGASSE

BEATRIX

nakirche

Makart- D

Wien Fluss

Sammlung
Religi ser
Volkskunst

SCHWARZENBERGSTR

Johann
Strauss- D

Stadtpark

Tierarztliche
Universit t

Kursalon

Wien

RECHTE BAHNGASSE

SCHUBERTRING

JOHANNESGASSE

LINKE BAHNGASSE

Beethoven- D

RNTNER RING

BEATRIXGASSE

K nstlerhaus

LOTHRINGER
STRASSE

Schwarzenberg- D

Konzerthaus

Akademietheater

SALESIANERGASSE

M nsikverein

AM HEUMARKT

Am Modena-
park

ahms- D

Historisches
Museum der
Stadt Wien

TRAUNGASSE

NEULINGGASSE

LSPLATZ

SCHWARZEN-
BERGPLATZ

ZAUNER-

GASSE

Schloss-
Belvedere

D                          E                          F

*The site of Peterskirche has been a Christian sanctuary since Roman times*

---

🕂 35E3
✉ Stubenring 5
☎ 711 360
🕐 Tue–Wed, Fri–Sun 10–6, Thu 10–9
🍴 Café (££) (➤ 93)
🚇 Stubentor
🚊 1, 2
♿ Good
💰 Moderate
↔ Stephansdom (➤ 26)
❓ Tours; audio guide; special exhibitions, often avant-garde

---

🕂 34C4
✉ Petersplatz 6
☎ 533 6433
🕐 Mon–Fri 6AM–6:30PM; Sat–Sun 7:30–6:30
🚇 Stephansplatz
🚌 Hopper 2A
♿ None
💰 Free
↔ Obizzi-Palais (➤ 33), Stephansdom (➤ 26)

---

## ÖSTERREICHISCHES MUSEUM FÜR ANGEWANDTE KUNST (MUSEUM OF APPLIED ART) ✪✪

The museum, often abbreviated to its initials (MAK), is one of the city's most enterprising institutions. Inspired by the Victoria and Albert Museum in London, it was founded in 1864 and moved into purpose-built premises, designed in a neo-Renaissance style in 1871. The collections include Italian majolica, Meissen porcelain, oriental carpets, textiles, Venetian glass, Biedermeier furniture, Judgendstil jewellery, metalwork and fashion items by leading artists of the trailblazing Wiener Werkstätte (Vienna Workshops). The museum was given a complete overhaul in 1993 when leading designers were given *carte blanche* to recreate individual rooms. It's all extremely stimulating and, when you've finished, there's the MAK café, one of the best known meeting places in Vienna.

## PETERSKIRCHE ✪

The baroque Peterskirche was completed in 1733 by Lukas Hildebrandt, better known as the architect of Schloss Belvedere (➤ 39). It can't have been easy designing a building to fit into such a narrow space but the site was an important one – this is where the first Christian church stood in Roman times. Inside as well as out, the most obvious feature is the dome, though sadly the ceiling frescoes have faded so badly that they're barely visible at all from ground level. More arresting is Enzo Mattielli's monument to the martyrdom of St John Nepomuk (according to legend he was hurled into the Vltava from the Charles Bridge in Prague). The *trompe l'oeil* effects in the choir are the work of Antonio Galli-Bibiena, famous in his day for illusionistic stage sets.

# Vienna

*From Stephansplatz cross Stock-im-Eisen-Platz.*

On arriving in Vienna apprentice metalsmiths would hammer a nail into a tree trunk for luck, hence Stock-im-Eisen (nail-studded stump).

*Stroll up the Graben, with its splendid 19th-century buildings, passing the exuberant Plague Column, erected in 1693, and the Peterskirche (► 36). Turn left into Kohlmarkt, with Demel's patisseries (► 92) on your right.*

At the end of Kohlmarkt, the classical façade of the Michaelerkirche contrasts with its simple Gothic interior. The grisly remains of wealthy parishioners can be seen in open coffins in the crypt.

*From Michaelerplatz take Schauflergasse, turning right into Minoritenplatz. Beyond the 14th-century Minoritenkirche turn left at Bankgasse to the Burgtheater.*

Part of the Ringstrasse project, initiated in 1857, the Burgtheater and the neo-Gothic Rathaus opposite are typical of the over-blown architecture of the late imperial period. On the corner of Dr-Karl-Lueger-Ring is Café Landtmann, where you can ponder the wonders of 19th-century town planning over a leisurely lunch.

*Walk past the theatre, then through the rose gardens of the Volksgarten. At the end is the Hofburg (► 32). Continue to Burg Tor. On your right is the Kunsthistorisches Museum (► 21). Turn left and walk through to the Inner Courtyard, then turn right under the Schweizer Tor to Josefsplatz, the entrance to the Spanish Riding School (► 44) and the Augustinerkirche. Walk down Augustinerstrasse, then turn left into Tegetthofstrasse and Neuer Markt.*

On the corner of the square is the Kapuzinergruft (► 33) while in the centre stands a copy of Georg Raphael Donner's splendid Providence Fountain of 1739. The original is in Schloss Belvedere (► 39).

*Time for a coffee on the Graben, Vienna's main shopping street*

**Distance**
2.5km

**Time**
2–6 hours depending on which sights you visit

**Start point**
Stephansplatz
⊞ 35D3
🚇 Stephansdom

**Finish point**
Neuer Markt
⊞ 34C2
🚇 Oper

**Lunch**
Café Landtmann (££), ► 92)
✉ 4 Dr-Karl-Lueger-Ring
☎ 532 0621

*The world-famous ferris wheel in the Prater*

🔢 35F5

🕐 Prater Funfair: Mar–Oct
8AM–midnight; ferris
wheel May–Sep
9AM–midnight; other
times 10–6

🍴 Cafés and restaurant
(£–££)

🚇 (Park) Praterstern;
(Danube) Alt Donau,
Donauinsel

✋ Entrance to park free;
attractions (including
ferris wheel) moderate.

❓ Danube excursions:
DDSG (Danube
Steamship Company)
✉ Friedrichstrasse 7
☎ 588 800

## PRATER AND THE DANUBE ⭐

The Prater – Latin for meadow – was an imperial hunting ground long before Emperor Josef II presented it to the people of Vienna in 1766 as a 'place of entertainment'. So it's in keeping with his wishes that the main attraction of the park is the fairground, a traditional affair with bumper cars, helter-skelter rides, a ghost train, side stalls, slot machines, shooting ranges and a good old-fashioned merry-go-round. If the fair doesn't appeal, you can take a stroll along the 5km chestnut avenue known as the Hauptallee, go cycling along one of the marked paths or explore the wooded areas of the park.

To the Viennese, the Prater is synonymous with the Riesenrad, a giant ferris wheel erected by British engineer Walter Basset in 1897. There are unbeatable views of Vienna from the wooden cabins as you climb to a maximum height of 64.7m. (The wheel turns at only 0.75 metres a second so there's plenty of time to take photographs.)

From the Prater it's no distance at all to the River Danube. Once you've seen it, it's impossible to confuse with the much narrower Danube Canal which skirts the inner city. The river – far from 'blue' incidentally – is artificially parted by a 21km strip of land called Danube Island. The best recreational facilities are at Donau Park where you can hire boats or take a cruise in summer.

---

### DID YOU KNOW?

The unforgettable encounter between Holly Martins (played by Joseph Cotton) and the enigmatic Harry Lime (Orson Welles) in the 1949 film classic *The Third Man*, directed by Carol Reed, takes place on the ferris wheel in the Prater. Nearly 40 years later, in 1987, the park was used again as a film set, this time for the James Bond movie *The Living Daylights*.

## SCHLOSS BELVEDERE ✪✪✪

This imposing baroque residence was built in 1714–23 for the great Austrian general, Prince Eugène of Savoy. There are actually two palaces, the Unteres (Lower) and Oberes (Upper) Belvedere, connected by a sloping formal garden: Lukas Hildebrandt designed them both. After the prince's death, Schloss Belvedere was acquired by the Hapsburgs. The last occupant was Archduke Franz-Ferdinand, who lived here from 1897 until his assassination in 1914.

Schloss Belvedere has several compelling art collections. In the Lower Palace you'll find an exhibition of Austrian baroque paintings and sculptures. Georg Donner's splendid fountain, copied at the Neuer Markt, is also worthy of note as is the grimacing bust by Franz Messerschmidt in the Grotesque Room. There's a wonderful collection of medieval art in the Orangerie. The Znaim altarpiece (c1400) is a gem and there are late Gothic masterpieces by Conrad Laib and Michael Pacher.

From here it's a gentle stroll to the Upper Palace and its fabulous collection of 19th- and 20th-century paintings, including – if they're not on loan – works by Monet, Manet, Degas, Renoir and Van Gogh. There are Expressionist works by Egon Schiele and Oskar Kokoschka, while the Austrian Secessionist school is represented by Gustav Klimt. As you leave the Belvedere, have your camera ready for the views of the Vienna skyline.

## SCHLOSS SCHÖNBRUNN (▶ 24–5, TOP TEN)

➕ 35D1
✉ Lower Belvedere, Orangery: Rennweg 6A; Upper Belvedere: Prinz-Eugen-Strasse 27
☎ 79 5570
🕐 Tue–Sun 10–5. Gardens 6AM–dusk
🍴 Café/restaurant (££)
🚍 71 (Lower Belvedere), D (Upper Belvedere)
♿ Good
🗓 Moderate

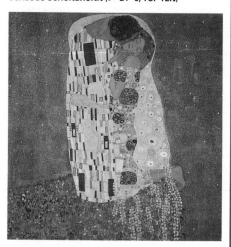

*Secessionist masterpiece – Gustav Klimt's* The Kiss *(1908)*

# Food & Drink

Austrians love their food but with the emphasis on *güte bürger-liche küche* – loosely translated as nourishing, hearty fare – rather than *haute cuisine*. Meat is the staple of the traditional diet, cooked in rich cream or wine sauces and served up with generous helpings of potatoes, dumplings and sauerkraut (pickled cabbage). However, healthier, more sensible eating is catching on, especially among the young, and nowadays most kitchens place greater emphasis on quality over quantity.

Austria's imperial past and her location at the heart of Europe account for the surprising diversity of the national cuisine. In Burgenland for example, *goulash* (paprika-flavoured beef stew), and *letscho* (stewed tomatoes mixed with spices and green pepper) are reminders that until the 1920s this region belonged to Hungary. Further south in Styria, Balkan influences make themselves felt in dishes such as *Bohnensuppe*, a spicy bean soup, and *Cevapcici* (rissoles cooked in a piquant tomato sauce). Styria's homegrown specialities include *Steirisches Wurzelfleisch* (pork cooked with root vegetables) and you should certainly try *Kurbisöl* (pumpkin seed oil) on salads. Dumplings originated in Bohemia and Upper Austria is still sometimes referred to as 'dumpling land'. Look out especially for *Semmelknödel*, bread crumbs soaked in milk and mixed with flour, egg, herbs and spices. A Tirolean variant, *Nockerl*, is made with a white cheese dough and flavoured with bacon or spinach. The 'national' dish of the Tirol is *Gröstel*, a delicious pan-fried offering prepared with sliced potatoes,

*Wienerschnitzel, often served with salad and potato salad, is a mainstay of Austrian cuisine – and portions can be huge*

pork, onions and spices. In Vienna you can try all of these dishes, not forgetting of course *Wienerschnitzel* (veal or pork cutlet fried in breadcrumbs). The quintessential Viennese dish is *Tafelspitz*, boiled fillet of beef served with potatoes and horseradish sauce – a favourite with the Emperor Franz-Josef.

*A stop at the pastry counter is a must*

## Wine

Austria is a major producer of excellent wines. *Veltliner*, made from the Grüner Veltliner grape, is the country's best known white wine. Dry, fragrant and a touch spicy, it's best encountered in a *Heuriger* (wine tavern). *Welschriesling* is fruitier, though decidedly inferior to *Rheinriesling*, produced in the Wachau. The best known red wine is *Blaufränkisch* – dry and highly palatable it goes very well with meat dishes. *Zweigelt*, also dry, has a bit more body. Even better is the muscat-flavoured *St Laurent* or, if you happen to be in Burgenland, *Esterházy*, a superb wine still produced on the Eisenstadt estate.

*By tradition, Sachertorte was invented by the chef of Vienna's Hotel Sacher, although the Hotel Imperial disputes that claim*

## Desserts

Forget watching your waistline and throw caution to the winds – Austrian puddings are an art form. *Apfelstrudel* (apples and raisins, wrapped in pastry and sprinkled with icing sugar) goes down a treat, as does *Sachertorte*, a wickedly rich chocolate gâteau with a layer of apricot jam under its chocolate icing. Other popular desserts include *Topfentorte* (cheesecake), *Palatschinken* (pancakes, usally with fruit or jam fillings), *Mohr in Hemd* ('Moor in a shirt', a chocolate pudding with sauce and whipped cream) or – Mozart's favourite – *Salzburger Nockerln*, a sweet egg soufflé flavoured with vanilla and icing sugar.

### SERVITENKIRCHE ✪

⊕ 34B6
✉ Servitengasse 9
☎ 346 195
🕐 8AM–10PM
🍴 Café nearby (£–££)
🚇 Rossauer Lände
🚊 Tram D
♿ Very good
💷 Free
↔ Sigmund Freud Museum (▶ 43)

Arguably the most appealing of Vienna's baroque churches – and one of only a few to predate the Turkish siege of 1683 – the Servitenkirche was commissioned by Prince Octavio Piccolomini in 1651, although the lavish interior was not completed for another 25 years. The architect, Carlo Canevale, was an Italian, as were the artists responsible for the magnificent stucco work. The frescoes in the cupola are equally eyecatching. The nave, unusual for its oval design, is separated from the entrance by a wrought iron gate. On your way out take a look at the black marble chapel of St Peregrine, patron saint of foot ailments. (The composer Joseph Haydn was among those who sought his help.) If the church has taken you a little out of your way, this is a quiet neighbourhood to relax in – there are tree-shaded benches in the square outside the church and a café just across the street.

*The Sezession building was deliberately designed to be provocative*

### SEZESSION ✪✪

⊕ 34C1
✉ Friedrichstrasse 12
☎ 587 5307
🕐 Tue–Sat 10–6, Sun/holidays 10–4
🚇 Karlsplatz
🚌 59A
↔ Kunsthistorisches Museum (▶ 21)
💷 Cheap
❓ Guided tours Sun 11:00

In 1897 a group of rebel artists, led by Gustav Klimt, 'seceded' from the conservative Viennese establishment to form their own association, based on the twin principles of freedom of expression and 'art for art's sake'. The Sezession building was designed for the staging of collaborative exhibitions by avant-garde artists, architects and designers with the aim of creating a *Gesamtkunstwerk* or 'total' work of art. Joseph Maria Olbrich's building, still striking despite being almost cut off by the traffic diverted around Karlsplatz, cocks a snook at the Akademie der

Bildenden Künste (Academy of Fine Arts) over the road. It's the dome, gilded with intertwining laurel leaves (nicknamed the 'golden cabbage' by the Viennese) that immediately strikes visitors but there are numerous other playful details – medusa heads, protruding owls, even a pair of salamanders. The inscription above the entrance, translated as: 'To the age its art, to art its freedom,' neatly summarises the aims of the movement. Inside is Klimt's dazzling Beethoven frieze, originally intended for a temporary exhibition in 1902. Thirty-four metres long, it's an elaborate allegorical narrative based on a Wagnerian interpretation of the famous *Ninth Symphony*. The three sections are: 'Yearning for Happiness' (left wall), 'Hostile Powers' (centre) and 'Happiness Attained', or 'Ode to Joy' (right).

### SIGMUND FREUD MUSEUM

The father of psychoanalysis, Sigmund Freud lived and worked in this building in Vienna's ninth district from 1891 until his enforced emigration in 1938. It was here that he wrote his *Interpretation of Dreams*, here too that his patients – the subjects of the famous case histories – came for consultations and treatment. Only the waiting room is furnished as Freud left it (he took most of his belongings with him when he fled to England) but the exhibition includes home movies made in the 1930s as well as documents and photographs, labelled in English and German. You can see a few of the great man's personal possessions – his hat, coat and walking stick for example, and the library too has been preserved – it contains every book published on psychoanalysis before 1938!

34B6
Berggasse 19
319 1596
9–4 (Jul–Sep 9–6)
Schottentor
Tram D
Few
Moderate
Servitenkirche (➤ 42)

*Display at the Sigmund Freud Museum (left), and the patients' waiting room (above)*

🗺 34C3
✉ Josefplatz
☎ 533 90310
🕐 Performances: Feb–Jun,
   Sep–Oct Sun 10:45 and
   some evenings.
   Rehearsals: Tue–Sat
   10–12 except late
   Jun–end of Aug when
   company may be on tour
Ⓤ Herrengasse
🚌 Hopper 3A to
   Hapsburggasse
♿ Few
💰 Expensive
↔ Hofburg (► 32)
❓ Tickets for rehearsals
   sold on the day at
   Josefplatz Tor 2; to
   reserve seats for
   performances write
   directly or book through a
   travel agent

*The decor of the Spanish
Riding School resembles
an elegant drawing room
rather than a dressage ring*

## SPANISCHE REITSCHULE (SPANISH RIDING SCHOOL)

This famous equestrian arena was designed in 1735 by Fischer von Erlach the Younger. The more prosaic title of Winter Riding School has never caught on with visitors who prefer 'Spanish', Spain being the country where the famous Lippizaner stallions originated. The training in deportment (dressage) was originally a sideline; it was their potential as cavalry horses that persuaded Archduke Karl to breed the beautiful silver-white creatures at his stud farms near Trieste.

Performances (*Vorführungen*) are held once or twice a week and last about an hour. Before 1918 the general public was excluded altogether; nowadays it's getting hold of tickets that's the problem. Each balletic routine is accompanied by music – polkas, waltzes, quadrilles etc – and the displays of horsemanship demonstrated by the riders are as immaculate as their dress (chocolate-coloured frock coats and two-cornered hats). Among the most spectacular manoeuvres are the *Levade*, in which the horse rears up slowly, placing its entire weight on its hind quarters; the *Courbette* where the same position is adopted before the stallion makes a series of jumps without touching the ground with its forelegs; and the *Capriole*, a leap during which the horse extends its hind as well as its front legs.

Most performances are sold out weeks in advance, but it is easier – and cheaper – to get into a rehearsal (*Morgenarbeit*). While there's no music, you'll be able to watch the horses being put through their paces and have a chance to admire the striking interior: white throughout with marble columns, chandeliers and a stucco ceiling.

> ### DID YOU KNOW?
>
> Only a few months before Crown Prince Rudolf committed suicide with his lover, Maria Vetsera, he had suggested a similar pact to another of his mistresses, Mizzi Caspar. She turned him down. What drove Rudolf to this ultimate act of despair is still a matter of controversy - one explanation is the Pope's refusal to annul his marriage, another is that he may have been suffering from syphilis, incurable in those days.

STEPHANSDOM (► 26, TOP TEN)

# Wienerwald (Vienna Woods)

*Leave Vienna on Bundestrasse 17, turning right at signs to Mödling.*

This pretty old town was a favourite retreat of composers, including Beethoven, who wrote his *Missa Solemnis* while staying at 79 Hauptstrasse.

*Take Weinstrasse along the edge of vineyards to Gumpoldskirchen.*

Vintners' courtyard houses line the main street of this wine-producing village. One of the best places to sample the excellent local whites is the characterful, old inn, Altes Zechhaus.

*Continue to the spa town of Baden (▶ 50). Leave on Bundestrasse 210.*

This scenic road follows the river Schwechal through the Helenental Valley, past the ruins of two medieval castles – Rauhenstein and Rauheneck – to Mayerling. It was here in 1889 that Crown Prince Rudolf committed suicide with his mistress, Maria Vetsera (▶ box opposite). The site of the hunting lodge is now marked by a neo-Gothic chapel.

*Leave on route 11 to Heiligenkreuz Abbey.*

The spacious abbey church, founded by the Cistercian order in 1135, is a perfect blend Romanesque and Gothic styles. Look out for the choir stalls carved with busts of the saints. Outside, the 13th-century cloisters and other buildings complete the picture of monastic life.

*Continue to Gaaden, then turn onto the small road which crosses the A21 to Sulz im Wienerwald. Turn right onto route 12 to skirt the Naturpark Sparbach, then turn again at the signs to 'Perchtoldsdorf Zentrum'.*

The Türkenmuseum in Perchtoldsdorf town hall and the massive fortified tower in the market square are reminders of the Ottoman incursions of the 16th and 17th centuries.

*Return to route 12 and continue to Vienna..*

**Distance**
80km

**Time**
6 hours with stops, 2 without

**Start/End Point**
Vienna
✛ 47C3

**Lunch**
Altes Zechhaus (££)
✉ Kirchenplatz 1,
   Gumpoldskirchen
☎ 02252 62247

*A typical carved wine barrel from the vineyards at Gumpoldskirchen*

# Eastern Austria

Eastern Austria consists of the provinces of Neiderösterreich (Lower Austria), Burgenland, Steiermark (Styria) and the Vienna basin. The Danube valley and its continuation, the Wachau, is wine country and you'll see vines growing on the slopes above the river. The scenery is idyllic and there's a great deal to visit: historic old towns, romantic castle ruins (the region's hallmark) and baroque churches perched on craggy promontories.

Burgenland, also famous for its vineyards, was part of Hungary until 1920 and the Magyar steppe is a characteristic feature of the countryside. The flat terrain around the serene reed-lake, Neusiedler See, is tailor-made for cyclists and birdwatchers. A political football, this eastern province was for centuries in the front line against the marauding Turks – hence Burgenland, 'land of castles'.

Any visit to Austria should include the second city, Graz, a lively university town with one of the best preserved old centres in Europe. The Styrians are an independent lot who speak their own dialect and are fiercely proud of their homeland.

> '*Whoever controls the Danube,
> controls all Europe.*'

ROMAN MAXIM

●

*Mariazell is Austria's leading centre of pilgrimage*

*The Schlossburg is Graz's most obvious landmark*

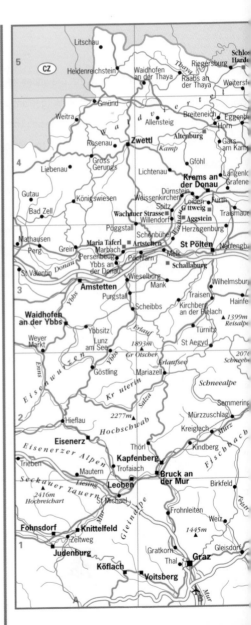

# EASTERN AUSTRIA

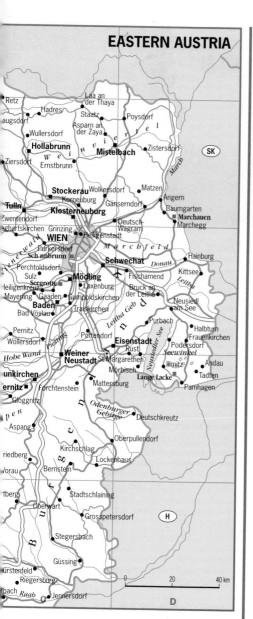

Retz
Hadres
Laa an
der Thaya
Staatz
augsdorf
Poysdorf
Wullersdorf
Asparn an
der Zaya
**Hollabrunn**
w e i n v i e r t e l
Ziersdorf
Ernstbrunn
**Mistelbach**
Zistersdorf
March
SK
**Stockerau** Wolkersdorf
Matzen
Korneuburg
Gänserndorf
Angern
**Tulln**
**Klosterneuburg**
Baumgarten
Zwentendorf
Deutsch-
**Marchauen**
ghartskirchen Grinzing
Wagram
**Marchegg**
Purkersdorf Heiligenstadt
**WIEN**
M a r c h f e l d
**Schönbrunn**
**Schwechat** Donau
Hainburg
Perchtoldsdorf
Fischamend
Kittsee
Sulz
**Mödling** Laxenburg
Leitha
Heiligenkreuz
**Seegrotte**
Bruck an
der Leitha
Mayerling Gaaden Gumpoldskirchen
Neusiedl
am See
Traiskirchen
Bad Vöslau
Leitha Geb
n d
Pernitz
Purbach
Wöllersdorf
Pottendorf
**Eisenstadt**
Halbturn
Frauenkirchen
Hohe Wand
Piesting
**Wiener**
Rust
Podersdorf
**Neustadt** St Margarethen
Seewinkel
unkirchen
Mörbisch
Illmitz
Andau
ernitz
Forchtenstein
Mattersburg
**Lange Lacke**
Tadten
Gloggnitz
Pamhagen
p e n
Odenburger
Gebirge
Aspang
Deutschkreutz
Oberpullendorf
riedberg
Kirchschlag
Lockenhaus
Vorau
Bernstein
tberg
Stadtschlaining
Oberwart
Grosspetersdorf
H
Stegersbach
Güssing
ürstenfeld
Riegersburg
0    20    40 km
lbach Raab
Jennersdorf
D

*The spacious interior of
the basilica at Mariazell*

Above: *The casino at
Baden*

**Roman palace (Kaiservilla)**

Right: *Schloss Esterházy*

## BADEN  ⚫⚫

This handsome spa town stands on the edge of the Wienerwald (Vienna Woods). For a time during the reign of Emperor Franz II (1792–1835) Baden was the official summer residence of the court, attracting dignitaries from all over Europe. It was especially popular with musicians: Mozart, Schubert, Brahms and the Strausses, father and son, all visited, while Beethoven returned year after year.

Life here proceeds at a sedate pace. You can visit the thermal baths or take a stroll through the elegant streets to enjoy the 19th-century Biedermeier architecture. When you're through with sightseeing, head for the beautiful surroundings of the Kurpark where there's a casino and an outdoor concert theatre .

## BRUCK AN DER LEITHA  ⚫

The River Leitha once marked the border between Austria and Hungary. Bruck itself is a pleasant, easy-going town and a convenient stopover if you're thinking of visiting Haydn's birthplace at Rohrau. From the baroque Hauptplatz it's a short walk to the attractive 18th-century parish church (pfarkirche). The castle was rebuilt in English Tudor style for the Harrach family in the 1850s and looks slightly the worse for wear. It's not open to the public but there's a nice ivy-clad restaurant with a shady courtyard on the edge of the grounds. From Bruck it's a short drive to Bruckneusdorf and the extensive ruins of a 34-room **Roman palace** begun in the reign of the Emperor Hadrian (2nd century AD).

## DÜRNSTEIN (➤ 16, TOP TEN)

## EISENSTADT ⊕⊕

This unassuming town is famous both for its wine and for its associations with the composer Joseph Haydn. Born in nearby Rohrau in 1732, Haydn entered the service of the Esterházy family in 1761 and remained with them for more than 40 years. Haydn's patron, Prince Nikolaus Esterházy, created a lavish and ostentatious court which, culturally at least, rivalled Vienna. **Schloss Esterházy** is the imposing baroque residence built for the family in the late 17th century (the towers allude to the medieval fortress which once occupied the site). Visitors are only allowed into the apartments on a guided tour conducted in German, but you can enjoy the frescoed ceiling and opulent surroundings of the 18th-century concert hall, the Haydnsaal, by attending one of the weekly concerts. Tours of the wine cellars are also available.

The modest house in which Haydn lived from 1766–88 and where he kept chickens and a couple of horses is now a **museum**. There's little in the way of period atmosphere, although you can see instruments played by members of the Esterházy orchestra and one of Haydn's organs.

Haydn's mortal remains now lie in the bloated baroque **Bergkirche**, where he regularly played the organ and where many of his masses were first performed. Completed in 1722, the church's main attraction is the extraordinary Kalvarienberg, in which the cross comprises 24 tableaux and more than 300 painted statues. There are great views of the countryside from the top.

47C3
✉ 45km south of Vienna
ℹ Schloss Esterházy
☎ 02682 67390
⬌ Neusiedler See (➤ 60), Bruck an der Leitha (➤ 50), Baden (➤ 50)

**Schloss Esterházy**
✉ Esterházy Platz
☎ 02682 719 3000
🕐 Mon–Fri 9–5 (Jul until 6)
🍴 Restaurant (££)
♿ None
💷 Moderate
❓ Concerts in Haydnsaal every weekend May–Oct; Haydntage festival Sep (➤ 112)

**Haydnmuseum**
✉ Joseph-Haydn-Gasse 21
☎ 02682 62652 29
🕐 Easter–Oct 9–12, 1–5
💷 Moderate

**Bergkirche**
✉ Haydnplatz 1
☎ 02682 62638
🕐 Apr–Oct 9–12, 1–5
💷 Moderate

*Downtown Graz is a maze of baroque courtyards*

🕂 46B1
✉ 140km southwest of Vienna
🚉 Graz
✈ Internal flights
ℹ Herrengasse 16
   ☎ 0316 8075
↔ Mur
❓ Tours of Schlossberg and old town (ask at tourist information office); Styriarte (Jun, Jul); Steirische Herbst (Oct) (▶ 112)

**Landeszeughaus**
✉ Herrengasse 16
☎ 0316 8017 4810
🕐 Mar–Oct Tue–Sun 9–5, Nov–6 Jan Tue–Sun 10–3
💰 Moderate

### GRAZ　✪✪✪

Austria's second city, Graz rivalled Vienna in importance until Ferdinand II moved his court to the capital early in the 17th century. The superb skyline of palatial Renaissance and baroque residences is very impressive, but Graz offers a great deal more than architecture. Apart from a host of musical and theatrical events, culminating in the contemporary international arts festival, Steirische Herbst (Styrian Autumn), Graz has its own 'Bermuda Triangle' of bars and restaurants, fuelled by a student population in excess of 40,000.

The Schlossberg is Graz's most obvious landmark. The castle was demolished in 1809 on the orders of Napoleon, leaving only the casemates and a couple of towers intact. The Kriegssteig, a flight of 260 stone steps, zig-zags up the hill to the Uhrturm (clock tower) or you can take the funicular. Look closely and you'll see that the hands on the brightly painted clockface have been swopped round. The Herberstein Gardens below have been planted with lemon and fig trees, pomegranate shrubs and wisterias. Look out over the terrace for panoramic views of the city. Near the top of the hill is the Glockenturm (bell tower). The bell, known as 'Lisl', was cast from 101 Turkish cannon balls.

The magnificent Landhaus was designed in 1557 by Domenico dell'Allio for the Styrian parliament. Look into the arcaded courtyard before going next door to the former Arsenal, the **Landeszeughaus** (note the martial statues of Mars and Bellona on either side of the doorway). Preserved almost exactly as it was in the 1640s, there are a staggering 30,000 exhibits here: swords, muskets, crossbows, suits of armour (including a full set of horse armour), cannons, powder horns and chain mail. For more than two centuries (1471–1689), Graz played a crucial role in the defence of Europe against the Turks. It was here that members of the Styrian levy were fitted out before being marched to the front. The Landeszeughaus is also a splendid architectural monument, best appreciated from the top of the building where there's a superb view across the courtyard towards the Schlossberg.

The 15th-century **Domkirche** (cathedral) has retained much of its original Gothic appearance. A faded medieval fresco on the south wall depicts the Turks as a scourge equal to the plague itself, while inside there's a 15th-century crucifixion by Konrad Laib. The extraordinary domed building alongside the cathedral is the mausoleum of Ferdinand II, designed by Pietro de Pomis in 1614. Ferdinand's tomb is to the right of the altar.

**Schloss Eggenberg** was the imposing baroque palace of one of Austria's most distinguished families. Also designed by Pietro de Pomis, it represents an elaborate allegory of universal order: four towers standing for the points on the compass, 365 windows for the days of the year, 24 state apartments for the hours of the day and so on. Peacocks preen themselves in the landscaped park where deer also roam. The most impressive of the Punkräume (State Apartments) is the Planetensaal (Planet Hall) with paintings by Styrian artist Hans Weissenkircher.

**Schloss Eggenberg**
- ✉ Eggenberger Allee 90
- ☎ 0316 583264
- 🕐 Park: Apr–Oct 8–7, Nov–Mar 8–5; apartments and museums: due to reopen in 2000
- 🍽 Restaurant (££)
- 🚇 1
- 🎫 Park: cheap

*Schloss Eggenberg was intended to symbolise universal harmony and order*

# Graz

*Flight of fancy – the clock tower on the Schlossberg*

**Distance**
3km

**Time**
2–4 hours depending on visits

**Start/End Point**
Hauptplatz

**Lunch**
Glockenspielkeller (££)
 Mehlplatz 3
☎ 0316 828701

*From Hauptplatz turn into Sackstrasse, lined with former residences of the Austrian nobility.*

Palais Khuenburg (no 18) was the birthplace of Archduke Franz-Ferdinand in 1863. The rococo Palais Herberstein (no 16, open to the public) belonged to the Eggenburg family, while the Counts of Attems lived in the baroque mansion opposite (no 17).

*At Schlossbergplatz climb the terraces to Schlossberg (➤ 52). Leave the hill via Sporgasse.*

This narrow shopping street also contains some fine historic houses – for example, the Renaissance 'Zur Goldenen Pastete' (no 28) and the Palais Saurau (no 25) – note the carved figure of a Turkish warrior under the cornice.

*Turn left into Hofgasse, passing the court bakery (➤ 104), the theatre and the town castle.*

The castle boasts an impressive double spiral staircase (1499) – look under the arch in the first courtyard.

*Cross to the Domkirche (➤ 53), then take the steps between the cathedral and mausoleum to Burgerstrasse. From here Abraham-St Clara Gasse leads to Glockenspielplatz.*

The celebrated musical clock entertains the crowds three times daily (11AM, 3PM and 6PM).

*Take Engegasse, then Stempfergasse to Herrengasse. Cross to the Landeszeughaus (➤ 52–3). Follow Landhausgasse past the heraldic arms of the old Styrian cities on the walls of the Landhaus. Turn right into Schmiedgasse and continue to Hauptplatz.*

The busy heart of Graz was first laid out in 1164 and still has its daily market. The most eyecatching of the façades surrounding the 19th-century town hall, is the richly stuccoed Luegghaus (corner of Sporgasse).

*The parish church of St Veit is decorated in true baroque extravaganza, with gold used lavishly everywhere*

## KREMS AN DER DONAU ✪✪✪

There are actually three communities here: Krems itself, Und and Stein. Once the seat of the Babenberg dukes, Krems has preserved a good deal of its architectural heritage, including the Steiner Tor (a monumental gateway and local landmark), the Renaissance town hall dating from 1491 and medieval burghers, houses in Landstrasse. As you explore the cobbled streets of the old centre look out for lively paintings of revellers on the façade of the Sgraffitohaus and the loggia of the Palais Gozzo in Hoher Markt. The local history museum (Weinstadtmuseum), housed in a former Dominican monastery, has exhibitions on the wine-making industry and other trades, and you can also visit the original 13th-century chapel and cloisters. A prolific 18th-century artist, Johann 'Kremser' Schmidt, decorated the ceiling of the dramatically baroque parish church of St Veit. Schmidt was also responsible for the frescoes in the church of St Nikolaus in Stein (see below) and the alterpiece in the Gothic Piaristenkirche (Church of the Order of Piarists).

The tourist office in the former Capuchin monastery in Und has an exhibition on the history of wine-making, although Und is better known for *Bailoni*, an apricot liqueur – many houses are decorated with fruit motifs. Surprisingly few visitors get as far as Stein, despite its charms, which include wonderful Renaissance façades, two picturesque salt barns and a former bishop's residence decorated with towers and crenellations. Art exhibitions are held in the 13th-century Minoritenkirche, now partly restored.

✚ 46B4
✉ 60km west of Vienna
🚏 Krems
🗂 Brandner Schiffahrt
    ✉ Ufer 50, Wallsee
    ☎ 07433 25900
    operates Danube cruises between Melk, Dürnstein and Krems
ℹ Undstrasse 6 ☎ 02732 82676
♿ Few
↔ Melk (➤ 23), Dürnstein (➤ 16), Mariazell (➤ 57)

# Weinviertel (Wine District)

**Distance**
200km

**Time**
9 hours (5 hours without stops)

**Start/End Point**
Vienna
 47C3

**Lunch**
Schlossgasthaus (££)
✉ Schloss Gatterburg, Retz
☎ 2942 2494
🕐 Closed Mon

**Österreichisches Motorradmuseum**
✉ Museumgasse, Eggenburg
🕐 Mon–Fri 8–4, Sat–Sun 10–5
💶 Cheap

*Bringing in the grape harvest in the Weinviertel*

*Take Bundestrasse 7 north from Vienna to Poysdorf.*

This town at the heart of the Weinviertel has been producing wine since the 14th century. It's a good place to see *Kellergassen* – rows of turf-covered wine cellars, usually on the edge of town. Some open their doors to prospective buyers who can sample the wines at a table in the *Presshaus* (cellar).

*Take the 219 to Staatz, then turn right on route 46 to Laa an der Thaya.*

Right on the border with the Czech Republic, Laa is not a town to linger in unless you're interested in beer – the Hubertus brewery has been supplying local inns since 1454. If you happen to be around in mid-September, take a look at the colourful Onion Festival.

*Take the 45 through Hadres to Haugsdorf. Continue to the junction with route 30, then turn right to Retz.*

Retz's windmill, set among vineyards at the edge of the town, is the local landmark. It's also famous for the red wines produced by the Weinbauschule. Beneath the picturesque town square is Austria's largest network of cellars, dating from the 15th century. Tours are organised from the Rathaus.

*Leave Retz on route 35 to Eggenburg.*

This ancient town has well-preserved walls, a church dating from the 12th century and a pillory in the Hauptplatz. For motorbike enthusiasts, the **Österreichisches Motorradmuseum**, with over 300 makes of bike displayed in a disused factory, is a must.

*Return to Vienna on Bundestrasse 303, turning off onto route 3 at Stockerau to avoid the Autobahn.*

## MARIAZELL ★

Famous as a place of pilgrimage, the **basilica** of Mariazell was founded by the Benedictines in 1157, but the shrine didn't acquire cult status until Louis I of Hungary attributed his victory over the Turks to the intervention of the Virgin of Mariazell in 1377. For believers, the focal point is the 12th-century statue of the Virgin, displayed behind a silver grille in the Gnadenkapelle (Miracles Chapel). The gorgeous high altar, by the great baroque master Fischer von Erlach the Elder, was commissioned by Emperor Charles VI. In the Schatzkammer (treasury) the *ex-votos*, dating back to medieval times, bear witness to the power of faith.

The world's oldest steam tramway runs (summer weekends only) between Mariazell and the pretty lake Erlaufsee. For walks and wonderful views of the Hochschwab mountains, take the **cable-car** to the Bürgeralpe (1,226m). Alternatively, drive to Hieflau, following the Salza ravine through forested and increasingly wild countryside.

## MELK (▶ 23, TOP TEN)

## MURTAL ★

One of the best ways to see the hilly, densely wooded Mur valley is to ride on the narrow-gauge railway that operates between Tamsweg in the Salzburger Land and Unzmarkt, west of Judenburg. The same company operates steam services in the summer with tourists in mind (trains connect Murau to Tamsweg or Stadl). Murau itself is a lovely town. It was founded by Ulrich of Liechtenstein, who built a castle here in the 13th century. Much of the town's medieval defences have survived, including parts of the old walls and the fortified town hall. The parish church dates from 1296 and contains some remarkable frescoes. Schloss Obermurau (rebuilt in the 17th century) looms over the fast-flowing river and the town, with its winding streets and timbered houses.

---

✚ 46B2
✉ 80km north of Graz
🚌 Dr-Leber-Strasse (centre). Services from Bruck and Graz

**Basilica**
🕐 Daily; Schatzkammer
🕐 May–Oct, Mon–Fri 10:30–12, 2–3 and weekends 10–3
↔ Krems (▶ 55), Dürnstein (▶ 16)
❓ Main events at the basilica are on major Marian feasts (15 Aug, 8 Sep) and at Whitsun
ℹ Hauptplatz 13
☎ 03882 2366
🚉 Mariazell-St Sebastian (15 mins)

**Cable-car to Bürgeralpe**
☎ 03882 2555
🕐 Jan–Jun, Oct–Nov 9–5; Jul–Aug 8:30–5:30; Sep 8:30–5; Dec 8–4
💶 Moderate

*Mariazell has been a seat of learning since the 12th century*

✚ 46A1
✉ 60km northwest of Graz
🚉 Murtalbahn ☎ 03532 2233 🕐 Daily; steam train Tue, Jun–mid-Sep, (and Sat in Aug)
ℹ Bahnhofplatz, Murau ☎ 03532 2720
↔ Graz (▶ 52)

# In the Know

If you have only a short time to visit Austria, or would like to get a real flavour of the country, here are some ideas:

## 10
## Ways to Be a Local

**Learn to yodel.** This has become something of an art form over the centuries (akin to singing) – you can even sign up for a course.

**Use the proper greeting.** Wherever you go in Austria, you'll be welcomed with the phrase *'Grüss Gott'*, a typical example of the famed Austrian hospitality, *Gemütlichkeit* (literally cosiness).

**Dress appropriately** – formal wear at the opera, smart clothes on Sunday and proper walking kit in the mountains.

**Go skiing.** More than half the population of Austria takes to the slopes every winter.

**Use the local transport.**

*Cafe Winkler, Salzburg*

Bus and train services are enviably efficient and are a good way of getting to know the area – you'll meet people too.

**Don't jay walk!** Always stop at a crossing and wait for the lights to change. Austrian people (especially the older generation) take this very seriously.

**Take the waters in a spa.** Despite, or maybe because of, their fondness for food and drink, Austrians are very health conscious and health is a regular topic of conversation.

**Go jogging.** Prater Park and the Danube islands are both popular with Viennese keep fit enthusiasts.

**Buy fresh bread** from the stall on the Graben in Vienna, or on Universitätzplatz in Salzburg.

**Shop for the traditional costume** – *lederhosen* (leather breeches) and *dirndls* (gathered skirts).

## 10
## Good Places to Have Lunch

**Winkler (££)** Outstanding views of Salzburg from the terrace.
✉ Am Mönchsberg, Salzburg ☎ 0662 847738

**Pfudl (££)** Famous for its *Beisl* cooking – the word is of Yiddish origin and implies plain, but honest, food served in unpretentious surroundings.
✉ Bäckerstrasse 22,

Vienna ☎ 512 6705

**Take a picnic** with you to the beach at Klagenfurt and enjoy wonderful views of the Wörther See.

**Berggasthof Rudolfsturm (£££)** Enjoy the regional specialities and the views over the Halstätter See.
✉ Salzberg 1, Hallstatt (Cable-car terminus) ☎ 06134 8253

**Alpenhotel Kaiser Franz-Joseph (££–£££)** Spectacular views of the Alps and the glacier – on a clear day you can see into Italy.
✉ Summit of Grossglockner ☎ 06542 7680

**Konditorei Kastmann (£)** Admire the famous golden roof from this café.
✉ Herzog-Friedrich-Strasse 9, Innsbruck

**See Restaurant (££)** Watch the boats set out onto the Neuseidler See while you enjoy Steckerl (a local fish, usually barbecued).
✉ Am Seekanal 2, Rust

**Landhauskeller (£££)** Enjoy a traditional Styrian lunch in the historic centre.
✉ Schmiedgasse 9, Graz ☎ 0316 830276

**Schweizerhaus (££)** Delicious haunches of meat in this garden-restaurant.
✉ Prater 116, Vienna ☎ 728 0152

**Gasthof zur Linde (££)** Specialities in game and locally caught trout.
✉ Laaben bei Leulengbach, Vienna Woods ☎ 02774 83780

*Left: Children hiking in the Wilder Kaiser, near Kufstein Right: Cable-car on its way up the Nordkette, Innsbruck*

# 5
## Top Activities

**Walking:** Many of the hills and mountain areas have well-marked paths and signposts giving you the distance and time to reach the next destination.

**Skiing,** or indeed snowboarding, tobogganning, ice skating and curling, at a top winter sports resort (➤ 114).

**Cycling:** Away from the mountains, this is one of the best ways of getting around and of enjoying the countryside on the thousands of miles of marked tracks.

**Swimming:** Austria has more than 2,000 lakes, many of which are well suited to swimming. The water in the Wörther See is enticingly warm, even in May.

**Rafting:** The fast flowing rivers of the Tirol are increasingly popular with rafting enthusiasts, but you'll need to take a local guide.

# 10
## Top Scenic Routes

• The train from Puchheim to Hallstatt follows the banks of the Traunsee to Bad Ischl and on to the Hallstätter See.

• The spectacular Semmering Pass between Mürzzuschlag and Gloggnitz was one of the first rail routes over the Alps, completed in 1854.

• The 30km run between Krems and Melk in the Wachau is one of the most scenic train journeys in Austria.

• En route to Innsbruck, the train from Zell am See climbs through the majestic Kitzbüheler Alpen before making the descent to the Inn valley.

• The boat cruise from Klagenfurt to Velden is a leisurely way of exploring the lakeside resorts of the Wörther See.

• The combination of funicular and two-stage cable-car ride from Innsbruck to the Hafelkar peak (2,334m) is the ideal way to view the Inn valley and surrounding countryside.

• The Murtalbahn narrow-gauge railway in the Mur valley runs a steam service between Unzmarkt and Tamsweg in summer (➤ 57).

• Motorists in the Paznauntal will enjoy the wonderful mountain drive on the Partenen to Galtür Road (also known as the Silvrettastrasse) – open May to Nov.

• There are breathtaking views of Bodensee from the cable-car to the summit of the Pfänder mountain (1,062m).

• The scenic steam railway from Mariazell goes to Erlaufsee, a pretty lake 3km to the northwest.

# 5
## Best Views

**Wachau Valley** from Burg Aggstein, 300m above the river.

**Vienna** from the giant ferris wheel in Prater, (➤ 38).

**Salzburg** from the terrace of the Hohensalzburg castle.

**The Danube** from Melk Abbey, perched on a bluff 50m above the river.

**The Loisach Valley and the Lechtal Alps** from Zugspitzkamm (2,805m), reached by cable-car from Obermoos.

*Rust is one of the prettier villages on the Neusiedler See*

➕ 47D3
📮 40km southeast of Vienna
📞 National Park, 02175 3442
🚉 Neusiedl am See, Purbach, Frauenkirchen
🚢 Mörbisch-Illmitz May–Oct 8:30–5 every 30mins
ℹ️ Schloss Esterházy, Eisenstadt ☎ 2682 63384; Hauptgasse 38, Purbach ☎ 02683 5920; Rathaus, Rust ☎ 02685 6475
♿ Few
🔁 Eisenstadt (▶ 51), Bruck an der Leitha (▶ 50), Baden (▶ 50)
❓ Seefestspiele, Mörbisch: tickets from Eisenstadt 02682 66210 or Mörbisch Seebühne (mid-Jun to end of Aug only) ☎ 02685 81810

## NEUSIEDLER SEE/SEEWINKEL NATIONALPARK ✪✪

This serene steppe lake, covering an area of about 320sq km, is the largest in Europe. Surrounded by vineyards and grassy plains, the screen of tall reedbeds is so dense in places that it's difficult to make out the water at all. Much of the region is now a national park, administered jointly by Austria and Hungary (▶ 12). While fully geared to tourism, environmental protection measures have ensured that Neusiedler See is not in any way spoilt. There's a host of activities on offer from swimming (the warm brackish water is nowhere more than about 2m deep) to sailing, windsurfing, hiking, tennis and golf. Cycling is especially encouraged: there are 1,000km of signposted tracks with rental and repair shops in almost every village.

If you're planning on staying in the area, give Neusiedl am See a wide berth in favour of Rust or Purbach. Rust is lively as well as pretty, the façades of its baroque and Renaissance houses painted in soft pastel colours. The main sight is the Fischerkirche, founded in the 12th century and enclosed within a protective wall to defend it against the Turks. The frescoes inside date back to the 14th century.

Purbach is a little more off the beaten track. Delightfully unpretentious, it boasts an entire street lined with grass-covered wine cellars, as well as many historic winegrowers' houses. At one time the Turks were almost permanently encamped outside the village. Parts of the defensive walls have survived, along with the Türkentor, a double gateway built in 1630–4. Purbach's most celebrated resident was the legendary 'Purbacher Turk': left behind by the retreating Ottoman army after getting drunk, he converted to Christianity and prospered.

Mörbisch is equally picturesque. You'll enjoy the Hofgassen (alleyways running off the main streets) where the houses are decorated with flowers and the traditional bunches of grain. Mörbisch is best known for the Seefestspiele, an operetta festival held on the largest floating stage in Europe (► 116).

*Viticulture is the mainstay of Purbach and neighbouring towns*

## WALDVIERTEL

'Forest district' appears something of a misnomer for this area of gently rolling countryside near the Czech frontier. The wonderful castles and monasteries of the region are best explored by car – Krems an der Donau (► 55) makes a good touring base. The glorious Benedictine abbey of Altenburg, with its lavishly decorated apartments and ceiling frescoes by Paul Troger, rates as the top attraction, followed by the romantic Cistercian monastery Stift Zwettl. The pick of the castles must be Heidenreichstein, a moated fortress with ramparts that have never been scaled by attackers. Also consider Schloss Hardegg and Rosenau, a rococo castle boasting Europe's only museum of freemasonry.

🚩 46B4
✉ 50km northwest of Vienna

**Stift Altenburg**
🕐 Apr–Oct tour 10, 11, 4
✋ Moderate

**Stift Zwettl**
🕐 Apr–Oct, Mon–Sat tour 10, 11, 2; Sun 11, 2, 3
✋ Moderate

**Heidenreichstein**
🕐 Apr–Oct, Tue–Sun tour hourly 2–4
✋ Moderate

# Central Austria

The central part of Austria includes Oberösterreich (Upper Austria), Kärnten (Carinthia), part of Steiermark (Styria) and most of Salzburger Land. Salzburg, regarded by many as one of the world's most beautiful cities, is, of course, synonymous with Mozart and the Salzburg Festival. Italianate in appearance, it's stolidly Germanic in character and conservative by nature. To the east is Austria's stunning lake district, the Salzkammergut – *salz* (salt) being the source of its wealth since prehistoric times. The brine spa at Bad Ischl became fashionable in the 19th century after Emperor Franz-Josef established his summer residence here.

Mahler, like Brahms, was inspired by the Carinthian lakes – don't be put off by the far-fetched misnomer 'Austrian Riviera', usually applied to the Wörther See, but only really true of Velden – the rest is quite unspoilt.

> *'The first day was so delightful, that I decided to stay for a second, and the second was so delightful that I have determined to stay for the time being.'*
>
> JOHANNES BRAHMS,
> on holiday in Carinthia (1877)

*Salzburg, the birthplace of Wolfgang Amadeus Mozart*

*Salzburg's Pferdshwemme (Horse Trough) is decorated appropriately with equine motifs*

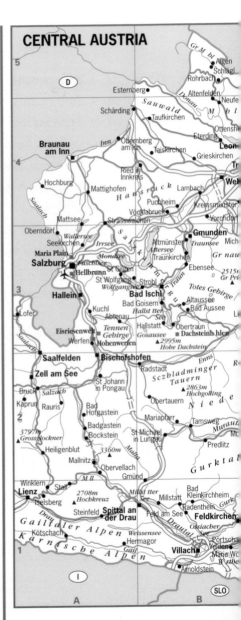

# CENTRAL AUSTRIA

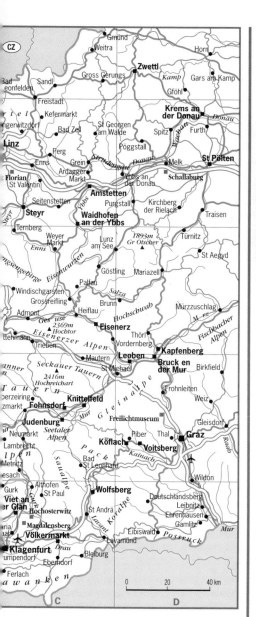

Composer Anton
Bruckner was organist at
St Florian Abbey, near
Linz in the mid-19th
century

➕ 64A3
✉ 225km west of Vienna
🚉 Salzburg
✈ Internal flights
ℹ Mozartplatz ☎ 0662 88987

*Salzburg, here seen from the Hohensalzburg fortress, is, architecturally, Austria's most Italianate city*

✉ Domplatz
☎ 0662 844189
🎫 Dommuseum (treasury) mid-May to mid-Oct Mon–Sat 10–5, Sun 11–5
💰 Donation
↔ Residenz (➤ 70), Franziskanerkirche (➤ 67), Peterskirche (➤ 70), Festung Hohensalzburg (➤ 67)
❓ Sung mass Sun 10am; organ recitals Jul–Sep Wed, Sat 11:15

# Salzburg

**One of Europe's most beautiful – and most conservative – cities, Salzburg spreads out along the banks of the Salzach river with the lower Alps beyond. Until 1816 Salzburg was an independent city state, ruled by prince-archbishops from the brooding Hohensalzburg fortress. One of them, Hieronymous von Colloredo, was the patron of Mozart, who was born here in 1756. Every year the Salzburg Festival (➤ 116) honours the composer in a feast of opera, orchestral music and theatre.**

## What to See in Salzburg

### DOMKIRCHE (CATHEDRAL)                                 ✪

When Salzburg's Romanesque basilica burned down in 1598, Archbishop Wolf Dietrich resolved to build a cathedral to rival St Peter's in Rome. His successor was less ambitious; even so, this magnificent church, designed by Italian architect Santino Solari and not completed until 1665, is one of the finest early baroque monuments north of the Alps. The beautifully proportioned façade, constructed from pink Untersberg marble, is matched by the spacious interior, crowned by an immense cupola. Mozart was baptised in the 12th-century font (note the four copper lions guarding the base); the composer would also have recognised the organ which dates from 1702–3.

The magnificent façade of Salzburg's cathedral is by Santino Solari

## FRANZISKANERKIRCHE (FRANCISCAN CHURCH) ✪

The Romanesque nave of the Franciscan church was adapted to harmonize with the lofty Gothic chancel, a forest of slender granite columns crowned by vaults added in the 15th century. The elaborate baroque altar, designed by Fischer von Erlach, contains a medieval madonna by the Tirolean sculptor, Michael Pacher.

## HOHENSALZBURG ✪✪✪

Founded in 1077, the fortress was substantially enlarged in the 16th century. There are panoramic views from the terrace near the Kuenburg Bastion (c1680). In the main courtyard look out for the cistern, dating from 1539, which stands beneath a lime tree nearly 350 years old. To visit the interior you'll need to sign up for the 40-minute guided tour. The State Apartments are the main attraction, notably the Golden Chamber, sumptuously decorated with gilded woodcarving and a gorgeous majolica stove. You also see the torture chamber, the prison cells and the hand-driven mechanical organ known as the Salzburg Steer (1502), for which Mozart's father composed chorales.

Five minutes' walk from the foot of the castle is the oldest convent in central Europe. **Stift Nonnberg** was founded in the 8th century and is a 'must see' for *Sound of Music* fans – it was here that Maria von Trapp tried her vocation as well as the patience of her Mother Superior! Inside there's a beautiful Gothic altar and medieval frescoes of St Rupert and Pope Gregory the Great.

✉ Franziskanergasse 5
☎ 0662 843629
🕐 Summer: 6:30AM–8PM; winter: 6:30AM–6PM
🔁 Peterskirche (➤ 70), Mozarts Geburtshaus (➤ 69), Resideuz (➤ 70)

✉ 120m above town
☎ 0662 84243011
🕐 Mid-Mar to mid-Jun 9–6; mid-Jun to mid-Sep 8:30–7; mid-Sep to mid-Mar 9–5
🍽 Restaurant (££)
🚠 Funicular: Jan–Apr, Oct–Dec 9–5; May–Sep 8AM–9PM (every 10 mins)
♿ Few
🎫 Moderate
🔁 Domkirche (➤ 66), Peterskirche (➤ 70)
❓ Concerts (ask at tourist information)

**Stift Nonnberg**
🕐 Autumn, spring 7–12, 1:30–5; summer till 7:30

67

# Salzburg

The gardens of Schloss Mirabell were laid out in 1690 by Fischer von Erlach. They can best be appreciated from the terrace at the top of the steps where Julie Andrews performed the Do-Re-Mi song in *The Sound of Music*.

*Walk down Schwarzstrasse, past the Mozart-Wohnhaus (➤ 69) to Staatsbrucke. Cross the River Salzach into Rathausplatz. Turn left onto Judengasse. Follow the road to the Waagplatz, then pass under the arch by St Michael's church into Residenzplatz.*

In the centre of the square is the 18th-century column to the Virgin Mary. Opposite the Residenz (➤ 70) is the Glockenspiel – performances daily at 11AM and 6PM.

*Cross Domplatz in front of the cathedral (➤ 66), then go through the arch into Kapitelplatz, where chess players challenge each other on a giant-sized board. At the top of the square you'll find the cable-car to Hohensalzburg (➤ 67). Walk through the cemetery of Peterskirche (➤ 70). From the church, cross the courtyard and turn left onto Franziskanergasse.*

Opposite the Franziskanerkirche (➤ 67) is the Rupertinum, a gallery of 20th-century art with a handful of paintings by Klimt and his contemporaries Kokoschka, Nolde and Kirchner.

*Continue on Franziskanergasse to Max-Reinhardtplatz, then take Hofstallgasse past the Festspielhaus to Herbert-von-Karajan-Platz.*

Here, under the sheer cliffs of the Mönchsberg, is an elaborate baroque horse trough, the Pferdschwemme.

*Turn into pedestrianised Getreidegasse, Salzburg's main shopping street, with the characteristic wrought-iron shop signs. At the end is Mozarts Gerburtshaus (➤ 69).*

*The formal gardens of Schloss Mirabell*

**Distance**
3km

**Time**
4 hours without visits to museums

**Start Point**
Mirabell Gardens

**End point**
Getreidegasse

**Lunch**
K+K am Waagplatz (££)
✉ Waagplatz 2
☎ 0662 842156

## MOZARTS GEBURTSHAUS
### (MOZART'S BIRTHPLACE)

It was on the third floor of this elegant apartment building that Salzburg's most famous son was born on 27 January 1756. While the museum is disappointingly short on atmosphere (only one of the rooms has been furnished as a 'typical bourgeois interior'), the personal effects, especially the miniature violin Mozart learnt to play as a child, have a particular fascination. As well as a lock of the composer's hair, his silk purse, tobacco case and ring, you can see an array of portraits, autograph letters and scores. The view across the courtyard towards the Kollegienkirche can't have changed much since Mozart's day.

Getreidegasse 9
0662 844313
9–6 (Jul, Aug 9–7)
Café Trzesniewski (ground floor) (£)
Moderate (combined ticket with Wohnhaus available).
Mozart-Wohnhaus (► below), Franziskaner-kirche (► 67)

*The façade of Mozarts Geburtshaus*

## MOZART-WOHNHAUS
### (THE MOZART RESIDENCE)

The eight room apartment the Mozart family rented from 1773–80 contains a fascinating exhibition which places the composer's life in context. Just pick up a headset and wander through the rooms, listening to the commentary which adjusts automatically. There are entertaining details concerning the Mozarts' domestic situation and of course their musical activities.

The exhibits include the pianoforte Mozart used for concerts and more homely items such as a tea and sugar box. Most of his early life was spent touring Europe; an inter-active video charts each of the main journeys and you can read what he thought of his fellow musicians by perusing the autograph letters.

Makartplatz 8
0662 874227
Daily 9–6 (Jul, Aug 9–7)
Moderate (combined ticket with Geburtshaus available)
Mozarts Geburtshaus (► above)

### DID YOU KNOW?

In 1917 three great artists, the poet Hugo von Hoffmansthal, the composer Richard Strauss and the producer Max Reinhard, met in the Café Tomasselli in Salzburg. During the conversation they discussed the idea of a Mozart Festival and three years later the first Salzburg Festival was held. Some of the world's greatest conductors have taken the stage here, including Herbert von Karajan, a native of the city who imposed his towering presence on the proceedings for more than 30 years.

69

St Peter Bezirk

0662 844576

Summer: 8–12:30, 2–8; rest of year 8–12:30, 2–6. Catacombs: May–Sep 10–5, Oct–Apr 10:30–3:30 (short guided tours on the hour)

Free (catacombs cheap)

Domkirche (► 66), Franziskanerkirche (► 67), Festung Hohensalzburg (► 67)

Residenzplatz 1

0662 840451

State Apartments: Jul–Aug 10–4:30, tours half–hourly; May–Jun, Sep–Oct, Dec, 10–12, 2–3, tours hourly; Jan–Apr, Nov, Mon–Fri 10–12, 2–3, tours hourly. Residenzgalerie: Apr–Sep 10–5; Oct–Mar, Thu–Tue 10–5

Moderate

Fürstenweg 37 (5km south of town)

0662 820 3720

Jul, Aug 9–7; May, Jun, Sep 9–5:30; Apr, Oct 9–4:30

Café (££)

55 from train station or Rathaus

Few

Expensive

Guided tours of Schloss/fountains

## PETERSKIRCHE

This 12th-century Romanesque basilica was given a thorough rococo facelift in the 1770s when the original wooden ceiling was replaced by baroque vaulting and the frescoes were whitewashed to make way for paintings by Caspar Memberger, Antonio Solari and others. The fabulous organ featured in the première of Mozart's C minor mass in 1783.

The churchyard is Salzburg's oldest (1627). Pressed against the hillside are the chapels, crypts and mausoleums of Salzburg's most illustrious families; Mozart's sister and Haydn's brother are also buried here. You can also visit the catacombs, a network of caves used as a cemetery by Christians in the 3rd century AD.

## RESIDENZ

Looking out onto the Residenzplatz is the palace of the Archbishop of Salzburg, founded in the 12th century and rebuilt in 1595–1619. The sumptuous State Apartments can be visited on a 50-minute guided tour which includes the Conference Hall where Mozart conducted the court orchestra. The Residenzgalerie houses the princely art collection, strong on 17th-century Dutch and Flemish painting. The most famous works are Rembrandt's *Old Woman Praying* and Rubens' *Allegory of Charles V as Master of the World.*

## SCHLOSS HELLBRUNN

This early baroque country estate was built for Prince-archbishop Markus Sittikus von Hohenems in 1613–19 by Santino Solari. Trick fountains, grottoes, fish ponds and a mechanical theatre operated by water are among the attractions of the beautiful landscaped gardens. There's also a folklore museum and a theatre but, if you have children with you, you might skip these in favour of the zoo. The more unusual animals include the alpine ibex, the snow leopard and the red panda, and there's a special area where children can stroke the animals.

*Schloss Hellbrunn was the perfect summer retreat for pleasure-loving Archbishop Markus Sittikus*

# What to See in Central Austria

### BAD ISCHL ●●

This handsome spa town became fashionable in the 19th century after Emperor Franz-Josef built a summer residence, the **Kaiservilla**, here in 1856. You can still recapture some of the town's faded imperial grandeur by strolling along the tree-shaded esplanade in the direction of the old pump room, known as the Trinkhalle. It was here that Franz-Josef signed the fateful declaration of war against Serbia in July 1914. The Emperor's wife, Elizabeth (Sisi) had her own palace in the beautifully landscaped Kaiserpark, now a museum of photography.

| | |
|---|---|
| ⊞ | 64B3 |
| ✉ | 40km southeast of Salzburg |
| 🚉 | Bad Ischl |
| ℹ | Bahnhofstrasse 6 |
| ☎ | 06132 277570 |
| ↔ | Gmunden (► 72), Hallstatt (► 18) |
| ❓ | Jul–Aug operetta festival |
| ☎ | 06132 23839 |

**Kaiservilla**
| | |
|---|---|
| ☎ | 06132 23241 |
| 🕐 | Guided tour May–Sep 9–11:45, 1–4:45 |
| 💰 | Moderate |

*Franz-Josef's summer residence at Bad Ischl*

---

> ### DID YOU KNOW?
>
> A great whirlwind romance began in Bad Ischl in the summer of 1853 when the young Emperor Franz-Josef fell in love with Princess Elizabeth of Bavaria and got engaged only three days after their first meeting. While the Emperor never regretted his impetuosity, the same cannot be said of Elizabeth, who quickly became estranged from her dutiful but reserved husband.

---

Franz-Josef was a regular patron of Zauner's pastry shop, birthplace of the delicious chocolate confection known as Zaunerstollen. Another famous café, Zammer's, was a favourite haunt of Brahms and Johann Strauss the Younger. Franz Léhar, who wrote the music to the operetta *The Merry Widow*, was so fond of Bad Ischl that he built a villa for himself on the banks of the Traun (now a museum).

### BRAUNAU-AM-INN ●

Shunned by many as the birthplace of Adolf Hitler, Braunau deserves a better fate. Surrounded by rolling countryside ideal for cycling, the picturesque little town lies just a few kilometres from the German border. The 100m high tower of the Gothic Stefanskirche is a local landmark. Part of the town's medieval walls also survive, notably the Torturm (Gate Tower) with its miniature carillon. The main square is lined with pastel-coloured burghers' houses dating from the 16–17th centuries.

| | |
|---|---|
| ⊞ | 64A4 |
| ✉ | 45km north of Salzburg |
| 🚉 | Braunau-am-Inn |
| ℹ | Stadtplatz 9 ☎ 07722 2644 |
| ↔ | Linz (► 76) |

### EISRIESENWELT (► 17, TOP TEN)

🔲 65C4
✉ 120km northeast of
Salzburg
🚂 Freistadt (3km)
ℹ Hauptplatz 12
☎ 07942 72974
↔ Linz (► 76)

## FREISTADT ⊙⊙

This delightful little town lies in the Muhlviertel, a region once famous for its mills. In medieval times Freistadt was an important border post on the salt route to Bohemia. Nowadays its remarkably preserved fortifications, dating from the 14th and 15th centuries, are a major tourist attraction. It will take you about half an hour to complete a circuit of the towers, gateways and double walls. Next, head for the Hauptplatz, the resplendent central square with pastel coloured baroque houses. On one side is the late-Gothic *Schloss*, now home to the Heimatmuseum (District Museum) which contains an unusual collection of painted glass. Of more general interest is the 15th-century Pfarrkirche (St Catherine's Church). It was given a baroque facelift but the original tower – a local landmark – survives. If you're here for more than a day you might consider driving over to Kefermarkt (11km) where the Wolfgangskirche has an exquisitely carved altarpiece dating from 1497. More than 40m high, it's rated as one of the finest in Europe.

🔲 64B3
🚂 Gmunden
🚢 *Gisela*,
Traunseeschiffahrt Eder
☎ 07612 5215
ℹ Am Graben 2 ☎ 07612
64305
↔ Hallstatt (► 18), Bad
Ischl (► 71)

**Cable-car**
✉ Freygasse 4
🕐 May–Aug 9–6; Sep 9–5;
Oct 9–4.30
💰 Expensive

## GMUNDEN ⊙⊙

This popular Salzkammergut resort has a lovely riverine setting at the northern tip of the Traunsee. Once the haunt of emperors – Kaiser Wilhelm II of Germany and Nicholas II of Russia to name but two – Gmunden continues to exude affluence and contentment. The focal point is the esplanade which runs along the lakefront towards the beach and harbour, where you can waterski and windsurf as well as sail. There are lake cruises on a 19th-century paddle-steamer, *Gisela*, which once carried the Emperor Franz-Josef; alternatively you could take a look at the 17th-century Landschloss before strolling across the wooden bridge to the 'castle-on-the-lake'.

Schloss Ort dates from the 15th century but was acquired in 1878 by an obscure Hapsburg, Archduke Salvator, who used the alias of Johann Ort before disappearing in South America. For stunning views take the **cable-car** to the top of the Grünberg (833m).

Each of Schloss
Hochosterwitz's 14 gates
was designed to present
a different challenge to
the Turkish invaders

## GURKTAL ★★

The Gurk valley is a charming region of lakes, hilltop castles and historic old towns like Villach, with its picturesque medieval centre, ruined *Schloss* and boat trips on the River Drau. Just to the north is the tranquil Ossiacher See and the holiday resort of Ossiach – home of the Carinthian Summer Music Festival. The main appeal of St Veit an der Glan lies in its Renaissance and baroque architecture, notably the splendid Rathaus (Town Hall), with its arcaded courtyard and state rooms, open for guided tours. No one travelling through the Gurktal should miss **Schloss Hochosterwitz**, the last word in fairy tale castles and the inspiration for Walt Disney's film *Snow White*. The 14 defensive gates were designed to withstand attacks from the Turks. You'll find more splendid military architecture in Friesach, an old fortress town with a medieval keep and walls partly intact. The main attraction in Gurk itself is the magnificent 12th-century Romanesque cathedral. For something different, visit the Zwergenpark with its comic garden statues and miniature railway (➤ 108).

### HALLSTATT (➤ 18, TOP TEN)

### HOHE TAUERN (➤ 19, TOP TEN)

✚ 64B1
✉ 25km north of Klagenfurt
🏠 Villach, St Veit
ℹ Dr Schnerich Strasse 12,
  Gurk ☎ 04266 812521
↔ Klagenfurt (➤ 75),
  Wörther See (➤ 22)

**Schloss Hochosterwitz**
🕐 Easter–Jun, Sep–Oct 9–5;
  Jul–Aug 8–6
✋ Moderate

Elegant properties line
the Traunsee at Gmunden

# The Upper Mur Valley

*Leave Klagenfurt on Bundestrasse 83, passing through the pretty medieval town of St Veit an der Glan on the way to Friesach.*

The oldest town in Carinthia, Friesach has retained much of its medieval fortifications, including a water-filled moat.

*Continue on route 83 to Neumarkt, then take the left turn to St Lambrecht (on the Lassnitz road).*

The imposing 14th-century monastery of St Lambrecht (look out for the twin-towered church) is worth a short stop. The major attraction is the baroque Stiftskirche (abbey church), while the Gothic-style Peterskirche across the courtyard makes a pleasing contrast.

*Charming Friesach is Carinthia's oldest town*

**Distance**
198km

**Time**
8 hours

**Start/End Point**
Klagenfurt
✛ 65C1

**Lunch**
Murau Brauhaus (£)
✉ Raffaltplatz 17
☎ 03532 2437

*Continue on the side road to picture-postcard Murau.*

There's enough here to keep you busy for an hour or two and, if it's not your turn at the wheel, a glass of the local brew (Murauer beer) will go down a treat. Murau has been producing beer for more than 500 years and the Brauhaus (brewery) has a restaurant, souvenir shop and small museum. If you're feeling energetic, climb the hill to the 17th-century Schloss Obermurau (closed to the public) and the 13th-century parish church with a fresco of St Anthony and his pig.

*From Murau follow the river westwards on Bundestrasse 97. Turn south at Stadl an der Mur, crossing the thickly forested slopes of the Gurktaler Alps to the junction with Bundestrasse 93. Turn left to Gurk (➤ 73). Continue on route 93 through Strassburg. At the junction with route 83 turn right to return to Klagenfurt.*

## KLAGENFURT ✪✪✪

This historic old town came into its own in 1518 when Maximilian I designated it the capital of Kärnten (Carinthia). Its beautifully preserved inner core, much of it pedestrianised, has won several awards and is worth at least half a day's exploration. Though not as lively as some resorts on the Wörther See, Klagenfurt is a convenient base for exploring the lake and the surrounding countryside and has attractions specially suited to children.

Klagenfurt's new town was laid out by Italian architects in the 16th century. Apart from some splendid municipal buildings, pride of place belongs to the impressive town houses with their arcaded courtyards. Neuer Platz is the focal point, the 16th-century Dragon Fountain being the star turn (the dragon is the town's emblem). In the Alter Platz, behind the Plague Column (1680) and the House of the Golden Goose (1489) is the twin-towered Landhaus (1590), former seat of the provincial assembly. Climb one of the arcaded staircases to the Wappensaal (Ceremonial Hall), emblazoned with the coats of arms of the Carinthian nobility. The cathedral, (Domkirche) was built by Protestants but handed over to the Jesuits who reconsecrated it in 1604.

To reach Wörther See (3km from town) take Villacherstrasse. On the way, you'll pass the popular Minimundus (► 108), a theme park containing scale models of the world's most famous buildings. Boat cruises explore the scenic Lendkanal, while trips on the lake itself leave from near the Strandbad (beach).

🏠 65C1

🔲 Klagenfurt

🚢 Lendkanal: mid-May to mid-Sep, further details from tourist office; Wörther See: Wörther See Schiffahrt ☎ 0463 21155

✈ Internal flights

ℹ Rathaus, Neuer Platz ☎ 0463 537223

↔ Wörther See (► 22), Gurktal (► 73)

*The unusual Dragon Fountain (Lindwurmbrunnen) dates from the 16th century*

### DID YOU KNOW?

Mahler composed his *Kindertotenlieder* (Songs on the Death of a Child) while vacationing at Maiernigg in 1901 and 1902. It was the time of his marriage to Alma Schindler and he had never been happier. Unfortunately, the music turned out to be prophetic. In 1907 his four-year-old daughter Maria Anna fell ill with diptheria and died.

Linz's main square is the perfect setting for a game of chess

➕ 65C4

✉ 90km northeast of Salzburg

🚊 Linz (2km)

ℹ Altes Rathaus, Hauptplatz 5 ☎ 0732 7070-1777

🔄 Stift St Florian (➤ 77), Steyr (➤ 77), Braunau-am-Inn (➤ 71)

**Neue Galerie**

✉ Blütenstrasse 15

☎ 0732 7070-3600

🕐 10–6, Thu 10–10

♿ Few

💶 Cheap

**Pöstlingbergbahn (narrow-gauge railway)**

✉ Urfahr

☎ 0732 7801-7002

🕐 Daily, every 20 mins

💶 Moderate (tickets from Tourist Information)

### LINZ ★

Linz's industrial heritage of steel and chemical plants sits uneasily with a more cultured past, recalled by Mozart's *Linz Symphony*, written on a visit here in 1783. (He stayed at Klostergasse 20, marked by a plaque.) Today it's a lively and interesting place where redevelopment and restoration have gone hand in hand to pleasing effect. Time your visit to coincide with the International Bruckner Festival in September and you'll be in for a musical treat (➤ 116).

If you're not planning on staying long, head straight for the **Neue Galerie** which has an outstanding collection of 20th-century Austrian paintings, including works by such luminaries as Klimt, Kokoschka, Schiele *et al*. Linz's Hauptplatz (Main Square) in the heart of the attractive Altstadt (Old Town) will stand comparison with any. The main points of interest here are the marble Trinity Column, erected in 1723; the Altes Rathaus (Old Town Hall), where Hitler met a frenzied reception on his 'homecoming' in March 1938; and the Alter Dom (Old Cathedral) erected by the Jesuits in the 1670s. If the weather's kind, there are panoramic views of the city from the Pöstlingberg, accessed by **narrow-gauge railway**.

**MARIA WÖRTH AND THE WÖRTHER SEE (➤ 22, TOP TEN)**

## STEYR ✪✪

A beautiful market town at the confluence of two rivers, Steyr wears its industrial past lightly. Its wealth stemmed from the iron ore mined in the Eisenerz mountains. Even today, the engines for BMWs are manufactured here. (Anyone interested in industrial history should visit the **Museum Industrielle Arbeitswelt**.) The old town, characterised by pastel-painted baroque frontages and gabled, red-tiled roofs, is a gem. One outstanding building deserves special mention: the three-storey Gothic Bummerlhaus, dating from 1497, was originally an inn. The town museum, in a 17th-century granary, has a typical sgraffitoed façade. Steyr also has proud musical associations: it was here that Schubert composed the *Trout Quintet* in 1819. If you're looking for an excursion, just to the west of town is the village of Christkindkl (Christ Child) where there's a post office for sending children's letters to Santa Claus and festive greetings to stamp collectors worldwide. Alternatively, go for a ride on a steam train to Grünberg (17km) on the **narrow-gauge railway**.

➕ 65C4
✉ 30km south of Linz
🚉 Steyr
ℹ Rathaus ✉ Stadtplatz 27 ☎ 07252 53229
↔ Stift St Florian (▶ below), Linz (▶ 76)

**Museum Industrielle Arbeitswelt**
✉ Wehrgrabengasse 7
☎ 07252 773510
🕐 Tue–Sun 10–5
💵 Moderate

**Steyrertalbahn (narrow-gauge railway)**
☎ 07252 46569
🕐 Weekends only Jun–Sep

## STIFT ST FLORIAN ✪✪✪

Stift St Florian and the surrounding countryside are dominated by a magnificent Augustinian abbey, founded in the 11th century. The monastery's baroque appearance dates from 1686–1751, when it was completely rebuilt: the Marmorsaal (Marble Hall) and Eagle Fountain are among the highlights. The ceiling frescoes in the library are by Almonte but also look out for works by the medieval master, Albrecht Altdorfer, in the gallery, particularly the magnificent Sebastian altarpiece (1518). The Stiftskirche (abbey church) is decorated almost to excess with *trompe l'oeil* frescoes, stucco mouldings and inventive wood carving (the choirstalls are worth a closer look). The church is particularly associated with the 19th-century composer, Anton Bruckner. A choirboy here, he was resident organist for more than 10 years and is buried in the crypt.

➕ 65C4
✉ 15km southeast of Linz
☎ 07224 8902-10
🕐 Guided tour only (1hr 30min) Apr–Oct 10, 11, 2, 3, 4
🍴 Restaurant (££)
💵 Moderate
↔ Linz (▶ 76), Steyr (▶ above)
❓ Summer concerts (Jun–Jul) ☎ 0732 776127

*Steyr's industrial past is not immediately obvious*

# Western Austria

The mountainous region of western Austria includes the provinces of Vorarlberg and Tirol and the western borders of Salzburger Land. Vorarlberg is a region apart, almost cut off from Austria proper by the barrier of the Alps and closer both geographically and culturally to Switzerland. Yet the capital, Bregenz, with the serene Bodensee on its doorstep, is only 8 hours by train from Vienna and the alpine scenery is as stunning here as anywhere in Austria. To most tourists, the Tirol means winter sports and ski resorts, but it's a summer destination too attracting hikers, climbers, cyclists and watersports enthusiasts. There's also Austria's highest peak, the Grossglockner, accessible via the famous mountain highway, and the gateway to the sublime Hohe Tauern National Park. The capital of the Tirol is the former imperial city of Innsbruck, an architectural treasure trove, cradled by snow-capped mountains.

> *Comme un morceau de ciel qui servirait de miroir à Dieu.*
> (Like a piece of sky which serves God as a mirror.)

ALEXANDRE DUMAS *père*,
about Bodensee (Lake Constance)

────────────●────────────

*Innsbruck Old Town*

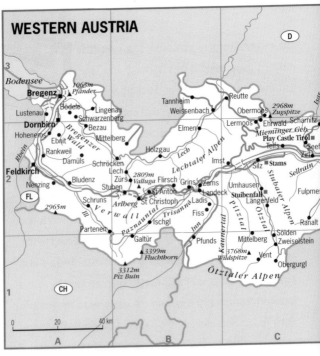

**WESTERN AUSTRIA**

🏛 81D2

📮 350km west of Vienna

🚉 Südtirolerplatz

ℹ Burggraben 3 ☎ 0512
535638

♿ Guide for Disabled
People available from
tourist information

🔁 Kitzbühel (►20), Öztaler
Alpen (►86), Zugspitze
(►90)

❓ Early Music Festival
(Aug); brass band
concerts (Goldenes
Dachl, May–Sep Sun
11:30; Tirolean evenings
(contact tourist
information)

## Innsbruck

With the stupendous Alpine backdrop of the
Nordkette virtually on its doorstep, the capital of
the Tirol must rank as one of the world's most
beautiful cities. Innsbruck leapt to prominence in

### DID YOU KNOW?

Despite making Innsbruck his capital and designing a
mausoleum for himself in the Hofkirche, Maximilian
I was to die an exile. Already terminally ill with cancer,
the weary emperor was forced to withdraw from the
city at the end of 1518 after the local innkeepers had
refused to admit his retinue, pending settlement of
outstanding debts. Maximilian eventually died in Wels
in January 1519 and was taken to his birthplace,
Wiener Neustadt, for burial.

Salzburg

Hallein

Kuchl

Kössen

Kaiser
Gebirge

Lofer

Steinernes

Salzach

Hügen Gebl.

Kufstein
Hintersteiner
See

Griesenau

St Johann
in Tirol

Lamprechtsofen
Höhle & Weissbach

Werfen

Inn

Achental

Rofan

Wörgl

Scheffau
Kitzbühel

1996m
▲Kitzbüheler
Horn

Meer

Saalach

Saalfelden

Bischofshofen

Achensee
Pertisau

Mauracn

Rattenberg

Westendorf

1655m
▲Hahnenkamm

St Johann
in Pongau

Jenbach

Kitzbüheler Alpen

Zell am See

Bruck

Karwendel

Unterinntal

Stans

Fügen

Alpbach

2334m
▲Hafelekar Inn

Schwaz

Ziller

Neukirchen

Salzach

Mittersill

Kaprun

Rauris

Bad

Innsbruck
▲Ambras
2246m
Patscherkofel

Zell am Ziller

Gerlos

Krimml
Krimmler
Fälle

Fusch

Ferleiten

Grossglockner
Hochalpenstrasse

Badgastein

Tuxer Alpen
Lanersbach

Brandberg

3797m
Grossglockner

Edelweiss
Spitze

Steinach

Hintertux

Mayrhofen

Franz-Josefs-
Höhe

Gletscherstrasse

Dornauberg

Zillertaler Alpen

Heiligenblut

chnitz

Brenner

Isel

Hohe

Tauern

Obervellach

Möll

3509m
Hochfeiler

Erlsbach

Matrei

Osttirol

Winklern

Stall

Defereggen
Gebirge

Lienz

Iselsberg

Drau

Oberdrauburg

Drau

Gailtaler Alpen

Gail

Kötschach

Karnische Alpen

I

D

E

F

the 1490s when Maximilian I designated it the imperial capital. Nowadays the city is known mainly for skiing, but you can enjoy the delights of the Old Town any time of year. Despite its small size, Innsbruck has a cosmopolitan feel and the nightlife is definitely worth exploring.

*Carriage rides are a thriving industry in Innsbruck*

*Herzog-Friedrich-Strasse, looking towards the Goldenes Dachl*

✉ Herzog-Friedrich-Strasse 15
☎ 0512 5281111
🕐 May–Sep 10–6, Oct–Apr Tue–Sun 10–12:30, 2–5
♿ Few
🎟 Moderate

✉ Rennweg
🕐 Daily

✉ Rennweg 1
☎ 0512 587186
🕐 Mon–Sat 9–5
♿ Few
🎟 Moderate

**Hofkirche**
✉ Universitätsstrasse 2
☎ 0512 584302
🕐 Mon–Sat 9–5
🎟 Cheap

## What to See in Innsbruck

### DOMKIRCHE ZU ST JAKOB (ST JACOB'S CATHEDRAL)    ❂

Innsbruck's lavish baroque cathedral was completed in 1724. The interior stucco decoration and ceiling frescoes are by two brothers, Egidius and Cosmas Damien Asam. Hidden among the fancy ornament over the high altar is the church's most famous artistic treasure, Lucas Cranach the Elder's *Madonna and Child* (1537).

### GOLDENES DACHL    ❂❂❂

Completed around 1500, the 'Golden Roof' is Innsbruck's most easily identifiable monument. Maximilian I's palace was intended to symbolise the power of the Hapsburgs, which would soon extend beyond Austria and the Netherlands to Spain and the New World. The ornate loggia is covered by a layer of gilded copper tiles which glint and dazzle in the sunlight. Maximilian liked to greet his subjects from the balcony before watching the entertainments staged in his honour below.

The Maximilianum is a small exhibition on the life of the Emperor, who, it turns out, was a mountaineer as well as an outstanding warrior and artistic patron.

### HOFBURG (IMPERIAL PALACE)    ❂❂

Rebuilt by Empress Maria Theresa in the 18th century, the Hofburg's main attractions are the Rococo apartments, although only the Riesesaal (Giant's Hall), with a ceiling fresco by the distiguished court painter Franz-Anton Maulbertsch, is exceptional. Better to focus your attention on Maximilian I's amazing mausoleum in the **Hofkirche** (Court Church) next door. The Renaissance marble tomb is surrounded by 28 larger than life bronze statues, representing the emperor's ancestors, real and imagined (England's King Arthur is among them). The figures were designed by Peter Vischer and Albrecht Dürer, a protégé of Maximilian's. The Silver Chapel, so called because of the silver madonna above the altar, contains the tomb of Archduke Ferdinand II.

# Exploring Innsbruck

The walk begins on Maria-Theresien-Strasse at the Annasäule, a column erected to commemorate Austria's defeat of the Bavarians on St Ann's Day in 1703. To the south you can see another piece of imperial bombast: the Triumphal Arch marked two events of 1765 – the death of Emperor Franz I and the marriage of Archduke Leopold II.

*Turn away from the arch and walk up Maria-Theresien-Strasse, Innsbruck's main shopping street. At the end, cross Marktgraben into the pedestrianised Old Town.*

Herzog-Friedrich-Strasse is lined with splendid town houses, replete with arcaded façades, oriel windows, wall paintings and carved Renaissance panels. The most eye-catching is the rococo Helblinghaus, festooned with stucco cherubs, scrolls, leaves and flowers. Opposite is the 14th-century watchtower known as the Stadtturm. Climb to the top for a bird's-eye view of the city.

*Follow the road to the left.*

Pass the historic Goldener Adler hotel (➤ 103) and continue to the River Inn and the Ottoburg, a corner house dating from 1494 (now a restaurant, ➤ 98).

*Return along Herzog-Friedrich Strasse, passing the Goldenes Dachl (➤ 82). Turn left, up Pfarrgasse to the cathedral (➤ 82). Return to Herzog-Friedrich Strasse, this time taking Hofgasse (left). Beyond the arch is Rennweg and the Hofburg complex (➤ 82).*

The entrance to the Hofkirche is through the **Tiroler Volkskunst-museum** (Tirolean Folk Art Museum). Among the colourful domestic bric-a-brac, reconstructed interiors, farming implements, costumes etc. are beautifully carved crib figures from the village of Thaur in the Inn Valley (the craftsmen are still at work today).

**Distance**
1km

**Time**
3hr with visits

**Start Point**
Annäsaule, Maria-Theresien-Strasse

**End**
Point Hofkirche, Universitätsstrasse

**Lunch**
Stiftskeller (££)
✉ Stiftgasse 1, by the Hofburg
☎ 0512 583490

**Tiroler Volkskunstmuseum**
🕐 Mon–Sat 9–5, Sun 9–12

*Rococo stucco work decorates the 18th-century Helblinghaus*

✚ 80B2
✉ 80km west of Innsbruck
ℹ Lech ☎ 05583 21610;
Arlberhaus, Anton
☎ 05446 22690

**Valluga cable-car**
☎ 05446 2352
🕐 Dec–early May, Jun–Sep
8:30–4:30

### ARLBERG ✪✪

The Arlberg massif marks the watershed between the Danube and the Rhine, dividing the people of the Vorarlberg from their eastern neighbours. Until recently this was an isolated part of the world – cars didn't make an appearance in the remoter spots until the 1940s. Nowadays the Arlberg is a popular, but exclusive, skiing area, patronised by royalty and commoners with matching incomes. Typically fashionable is St Anton, the largest resort in the area. Skiing revolves around the Valluga at 2,809m but the **cable-car** network also reaches the upper slopes of Galzig, Kapall and other peaks.

In 1978, a 14km-long road tunnel was built under the desolate Alberg Pass. The overland route from St Anton winds its way via St Christoph, where a local shepherd built a hospice for travellers in the 14th century. Ten

*Two of Austria's most popular ski resorts are in the Arlberg – Lech (above) and St Anton (right)*

kilometres to the west is Stuben, birthplace of the pioneer alpine skier Hannes Schneider and still a favourite with dedicated skiers. If your thoughts incline more to *après ski*, Lech rivals St Anton as the liveliest resort in the region. The pastoral setting is undeniably appealing and, besides skiing, boating, mountain biking, river rafting and cycling are all catered for, while anglers head for the Spüller or Zürser See. A few kilometres from Lech is Zürs, the most exclusive resort of all, nestling in the beautiful Flexen Pass at 1,700m.

*Capturing the sunset over the Bodensee at Bregenz – an irresistible challenge for photographers*

### BREGENZ ✪✪

The regional capital of the Vorarlberg is an elegant resort with a lovely situation overlooking Bodensee. At the beach there are swimming pools, a watersport harbour, a marina and the port from where boats leave for excursions on the lake – it's possible to visit Germany and Switzerland on a round trip if you have your passport with you.

Right on the quay is the imposing neo-classical post office; its foundations rest on wooden piles – most of the land in the lower town was reclaimed from the lake. Behind is the Nepomuk-Kapelle (sailor's chapel), Kornplatz with its weekly market, the Landesmuseum – good on Roman Bregenz – and the neo-Gothic Herz-Jesu church, with twin towers and striking modern stained glass. The upper town was founded around 1200 by Hugh de Montfort. The obvious landmark here is the Martinsturm, a medieval tower with an enormous onion dome unceremoniously grafted on in 1601.

For an overview of the lake and mountainscape, take the **cable-car** to the top of the Pfänder (1,064m) where it's said you can see 240 alpine peaks. There are several restaurants at the summit, as well as a free zoo and falconry displays.

The Bregenzerwald makes a good excursion – it's here that you're likely to see traditional Vorarlberg farmhouses with their distinctive wood-shingle roofs. Plan your itinerary to include Bezau, Damüls, Schröcken and Schwarzenberg.

✚ 80A3
✉ 130km west of Innsbruck
🚉 Bregenz
ℹ Banhofstrasse 14
☎ 05574 49590
❓ Bregenz Festival
mid–Jul–mid-Aug
(▶ 113, panel)

**Pfänderbahn (cable-car)**
✉ Belrupstrasse
🕐 Dec–Mar 9–6, Apr–Nov
9–7 every ½ hour

### KITZBÜHEL (▶ 20, TOP TEN)

### ÖTZTAL

The Ötztal is prime glacier-skiing country, with rock climbing, mountaineering and hiking also popular. Sölden, the 'capital' of the Upper Ötztal, is a major package resort offering summer as well as winter skiing and spectacular alpine views from the nearby peaks of Rotkogel and Galatschkogel. The steep road southwest of Zwieselstein leads to Vent, a tiny village in the shadow of the Wildspitze, the highest peak in the northern Tirol (3,774m). The other major skiing area lies south of Zwiesenstein in the Gurgtal. The popular winter sports centre of Obergurgl, Austria's highest village, has a more rustic flavour than Sölden although the facilities are comparable.

It was in the Ötztaler Alps, right on the border with Italy, that the mummified body of a 5,000 year old Neolithic trader, nicknamed 'Ötzi', was discovered in the early 1990s. At the other end of the Ötztal, the pretty resort of Umhausen is only an hour's walk from the dramatic Stuiben waterfall while Längenfeld's Pestkapelle (plague chapel) rivals the spa as an attraction for visitors. You could drive the entire length of the Ötztal on the St Leonhard In Passeier road, usually snow free even in the depths of winter.

### PAZNAUNTAL

The Paznaun is a densely wooded valley close to the Swiss border, best known for the ski resorts of Ischgl and Galtür. Package tourists are Ischgl's major source of income, winter travellers for the most part. In summer it's still relatively quiet, though for how much longer is

---

✚ 80C2
🚌 40km southwest of Innsbruck
ℹ Rindlhaus, Sölden
   ☎ 05254 22120
🚌 Ötztal

*Sölden, ski capital of the Ötztal, is now a major tourist resort all year round*

✚ 80B2
🚌 100km southwest of Innsbruck
ℹ Ischgl ☎ 05444 52660

anyone's guess. The most popular excursion is the cable car trip to the Idalpe (2,300m), with spectacular walks in the direction of the Swiss resort of Samnaun.

A few kilometres from Ischgl, the smaller resort of Galtür offers climbing opportunities as well as winter sports, including cross-country skiing. The Silvretta Hochalpenstrasse toll road above Galtür is usually open from mid-April to mid-September and makes an exhilarating drive. The route follows the valley of the Trisanna river, passing through the Bielerhöhe pass and the Silvretta lake (Vermunt-Staussee), where boat trips are possible.

*When the skiers depart, Ischgl offers rustic peace and quiet*

### UNTERINTAL ✪

The Inn valley to the east of Innsbruck is a region of great character and natural beauty. Most of the historic little towns here prospered from copper and silver mining in the 16th century. There's an underground **mining museum** beneath the Tuxer Alps at Schwaz. Rattenberg, just outside Brixlegg, is also famous for mining. Looming over the picturesque streets are the ruins of Maximilian I's old castle. Much better preserved is the Emperor's 'pleasure palace' of **Schloss Geroldseck** in Kufstein (near the German border) and Schloss Tratzberg, between Stans and Jenbach. Jenbach is also the home of the famous Riedel glassware factory and shop. A steam-driven cog railway runs towards Seespitz on the tranquil Achensee.

➕ 81D2
✉ 60km northeast of Innsbruck
ℹ Unterer Stadtplatz, Kufstein 8 ☎ 05372 62207
↔ Zillertal (➤ 90)

**Silberbergwerk (Silver Mine)**
✉ Alter Landstrasse 3A, Schwaz
☎ 05242 723720
🕐 Jan–mid-Nov 8:30–5; mid Nov–Dec 9:30–4
👜 Moderate

**Schloss Geroldseck**
✉ Kufstein
☎ 05372 62207
🕐 Castle: May–Oct 9–7, museum: May–Oct Tue–Sun, tours 9:30, 11, 1:30, 4:30
👜 Castle free, museum cheap

*Steam ride on the Achensee*

# Grossglockner Hochalpenstrasse (High Alpen Road)

*Leave Zell am See (➤ 89) on route 107. At Bruck, the toll gates signal the start of the mountain road.*

The road over the Grossglockner pass was built in 1930–35. An amazing feat of engineering, it's 48km long with 39 hairpin bends between Ferleiten and Fuscher Torl – a climb with a maximum gradient of 12 percent. There are numerous parking areas along the way, all with views, and there's an observation tower at Edelweissspitze. At the highest point, Hochtor (2,505m), the road enters a short tunnel and there are more stunning vistas as you emerge.

*The Grossglockner Highway must be one of the most scenic routes in the world*

**Distance**
86 km

**Time**
9 hours (3 hours without stops)

**Start Point**
Zell am See
➕ 81F2

**End Point**
Lienz
➕ 81F1

**Lunch**
Glocknerhof (££)
✉ Hof 3, Heiligenblut
☎ 04824 2244

🕓 Road open
May–beginning Nov,
5AM–10PM

*Beyond the tunnel take the twisting side turn known as the Gletscherstrasse, to Franz Josefs Höhe.*

There's a hotel with a restaurant and viewing terrace. A cable-car takes visitors down to the breathtaking Pasterze Glacier – flowing more than 10km, it's one of the most impressive in Europe.

*Continue on route 107 down the south side of the mountain to Heiligenblut.*

Nestling in the folds of the Hohe Tauern mountains, Heiligenblut is especially photogenic when the sun alights on the slender Gothic spire of the parish church. Take a look inside at the magnificent altarpiece: almost 11m high, it was carved by Wolfgang Hasslinger in 1520.

*Follow the River Moll to Winklern. From here, the road climbs the Iselsberg Pass (1,204m), before descending towards Lienz, offering fine views of the Lienz Dolomites and the town itself.*

## ZELL AM SEE ★★

With breathtaking mountain scenery and an amazing variety of sporting activities to hand, this charming lakeside resort can hardly fail to appeal. Skiing is the main winter activity – the pistes below the Schmittenhöhe (in Zell) and Kitzsteinhorn (in nearby Kaprun) are well suited to beginners and intermediate skiers. At high altitude, you get around by ski lift and cable car, while regular bus services link the resorts below.

Zell is the ideal place to learn new skills and experience new thrills: snowboarding, tobogganing, ice skating and curling for example. Glacier skiing is also possible in summer from Kaprun. Otherwise, when the landscape undergoes its seasonal transformation, the lake is taken over by sailors and windsurfers while the less energetic amble along to the beach.

There's not much to see in the town itself, apart from the medieval parish church. Boat trips across the lake to Thumersbach, which has its own beach, leave from the esplanade. For something more invigorating, take the **cable-car** up the Schmittenhöhe mountain where you can enjoy panoramic views of the Glockner and Tauern ranges from a 600m vantage point. From mid-May to October you can travel on the breathtaking alpine pass, the Grossglockner Hochalpenstrasse (► 88). Another 'must see' is the 400m high Krimml Waterfall – take the **Pinzgaubahn**, a narrow-gauge steam railway which winds its way unhurriedly through the flower-strewn meadows of the Salzach valley.

81F2
100km east of Innsbruck
Zell am See
Zell–Thumersbach
Brucker Bundesstrasse 1
☎ 06542 770
Hohe Tauern National Park (► 19), Kitzbühel (► 20)
Krampusläufen folk festival (Dec)

**Schmittenhöhe cable car**
Mid-May to mid-Oct 8:30–5; otherwise 8:30–4:30

**Pinzgauer**
Jul–Aug, Tue, Thu, Sat, Sun 9:15; Sep, Sat 9:15

*Local public transport, Zell am See*

81D2

40km southeast of Innsbruck

Innsbruck (► 80), Unterinntal (► 87)

**Mayrhofen**

Europahaus Congress Centre ☎ 05285 2305

Zillertalbahn ☎ 05244 63470 🕐 Daily (steam service twice daily Jun–Sep) 💷 Expensive

*Germany and Austria meet on the Zugspitze*

80C3

40km northwest of Innsbruck

Ehrwald (1km)

Kirchplatz 1, Ehrwald ☎ 05673 2395

Ehrwald (1km)

**Zugspitzbahn cable-car**

☎ 05673 2309

🕐 Mid-May–end Oct; Dec–mid-Apr 9–4:30

💷 Moderate

## ZILLERTAL ✪✪

The Ziller valley has become one of the most popular Austrian package destinations. Apart from skiing and other winter sports, it offers hiking, kayaking, paragliding, rafting and rock climbing, not to mention the scenery which, south of Mayrhofen, is spectacular.

The main centre is the Tirolean market town of Zell am Ziller where traditional rural customs are vigorously observed, typically in early May when thousands of visitors converge to witness the Gauderfest, a lively rural knees-up with folk music and dancing lubricated with locally brewed beer. Ten kilometres south of Zell is **Mayrhofen**, an unabashed tourist resort, especially popular with hikers. Mayrhofen is also the terminus of the Zillertalbahn, a narrow-gauge railway which operates some steam services along the Ziller valley to Jenbach.

Beyond Mayrhofen, a scenic mountain road connects the old Tirolean villages of the Tuxer valley, a summer glacier skiing region, very busy at the height of the season.

## ZUGSPITZE ✪✪

One of Austria's 'must do' experiences is the ascent to this majestic peak (2,964m) on the frontier between the Austrian and Bavarian Alps. The **Zugspitzbahn cable-car** leaves from Obermoos (4.5km from the ski resort of Ehrwald) for the viewing platform at Zugspitzkamm. From this vantage point you can look out over the pine forests of the Loisach valley and the Lechtal Alps. To reach the summit you'll need your passport as this is German territory. The views are positively breathtaking: on a clear day you can make out the Grossglockner glacier, the Stubai and Ziller Alps and, to the north, the Bavarian lowlands and lakes.

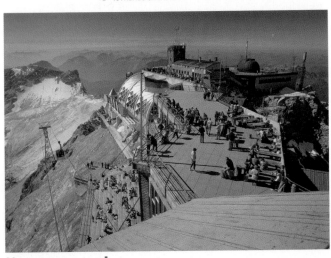

# Where To...

Above: *Village brass band*
Right: *The god of wine presides over Grinzing*

# Vienna

## Heurige

A *Heuriger* is what the Viennese call the current year's (*heuri*) wine harvest. It's also the term used for wine taverns in the villages of the Wienerwald which have their own gardens and often live *Schrammelmusik* (using a combination of instruments, including the fiddle, guitar and accordian). It was one of these *Heuriger* musicians, the zither player Anton Karas, who played the catchy Harry Lime theme in *The Third Man*.

## Achilleus (££)

First-rate Greek restaurant with well-presented *mezedaki* (starter plates), moussaka etc. The back room is decorated in the style of a Greek courtyard and has a bit more atmosphere.

✉ Köllnerhofgasse 3 ☎ 512 8328 🚇 Schwedenplatz

## Bach-Hengel (££)

The Hengel family has been associated with viticulture since 1137. This large *Heuriger*, is made up of cosy rooms and large halls, and there's a garden, of course.

✉ Sandgasse 7–9, Grinzing ☎ 320 2439 🚌 38

## Braunsperger (££)

Family-run *Heuriger* in one of the quieter suburbs with hot and cold buffet and a good selection of desserts. Wines include *Zweigelt* and the Danube speciality *Gemischter Satz*.

✉ Sieveringerstrasse 108, Sievering ☎ 320 3992 🚌 39a 🕐 Every odd month

## Café Central (£)

This turn-of-the-century café has retained its atmosphere of faded elegance. Leon Trotsky used to debate with revolutionary colleagues beneath the splendid vaulted ceiling.

✉ Herrengasse 14 ☎ 533 3763 🚇 Herrengasse

## Café Landtmann (££)

One of Vienna's best known and stylish cafés, Landtmann was Freud's favourite and is now frequented by politicians, actors and other glitterati.

✉ Dr-Karl-Lueger-Ring 4 ☎ 532 0621 🚇 Herrengasse

## Demel (£–££)

Celebrated café with gorgeous decor, smart service and a bewildering array of desserts. Try the *Burgtheater-Linzertorte*, shortcake flavoured with almonds and oranges.

✉ Kohlmarkt 14 ☎ 535 1717 🚇 Herrengasse

## Frauenhuber (££)

In the 18th century Frauenhuber was a concert hall (► 93, panel) but today it's a typical Viennese restaurant; slow-paced and sedate, but comfortable.

✉ Himmelpfortgasse 6 ☎ 512 4323 🚇 Stephansplatz

## Gulaschmuseum (£–££)

Excellent restaurant with a good central location. The goulash dishes include fish and are well worth waiting for.

✉ Schulerstrasse 20 ☎ 512 1017 🚇 Stephansplatz/Dr-Karl-Luger-Platz

## Hans Schmidt (££–£££)

Typical Viennese *Heuriger* on Grinzing's main street with a self-service buffet.

✉ Cobenzlgasse 38, Grinzing ☎ 326271 🚌 38

## Kierlinger (££)

An 18th-century *Heuriger* with wines cultivated on the Nussberg. Try the house speciality, Riesling-Traminer.

✉ Kahlenbergerstrasse 20, Nussdorf ☎ 372264 🕐 Closed Easter, Whitsun, mid–end Aug, mid–end Oct 🚊 Tram D

## Lale (££)

Deceptively Viennese in appearance, this popular Turkish restaurant offers a large range of chicken and lamb grills. No credit cards.

✉ Franz-Josef-Kai 29
☎ 535 2736 🚇 Swedenplatz

## MAK (£–££)

Popular with young(ish) trendies, the café in the Museum of Applied Art also serves meals and is especially hot on vegetarian and pasta dishes. Shady courtyard for cooling off in the summer months.

✉ Stubenring 3–5 ☎ 714 0121 🕐 Closed Mon
🚇 Stubentor

## Neu Wein (£££)

Fresh-faced, arty restaurant serving *nouvelle cuisine*. Try the *Zanderfilet*, pike perch, which comes with a creamy beet sauce. Booking essential.

✉ Bäckerstrasse 5 ☎ 512 0999 🕐 Dinner only. Closed weekends in summer
🚇 Stephansplatz

## Schweizerhaus (££)

This atmospheric garden-restaurant in the Prater has been here since the 1920s. Popular with the Viennese, you can watch the waiters carrying huge haunches of meat from the kitchen to the tables. *Schnitzels* (veal or port cutlet fried in breadcrumbs) and salads are available for the faint-hearted! Genuine Czech Budweiser on tap.

✉ Prater 116 ☎ 728 0152
🚇 Praterstern

## Steirereck (£££)

You'll need a collar and tie to be received in this, one of Austria's most highly rated (and expensive) restaurants. Excellent range of fish dishes including turbot and

also delicious quail. Booking essential.

✉ Rasumofskygasse 2
☎ 713 3168 🕐 Closed weekends 🚇 Rochusgasse

## Venezia (£–££)

Large, elegant pizzeria, just a stone's throw from St Stephen's Cathedral.

✉ Kärntnerstrasse 10
☎ 512 6234
🚇 Stephansplatz

## Weingut Reinprecht (££–£££)

Typical *Heuriger* with Viennese music, home-grown wines, self-service buffet and terrace garden.

✉ Cobenzlgasse 22, Grinzing
☎ 320 14710 🕐 Mar–Nov
🚌 38

## Weinhof Gstaltner (££)

This family *Heuriger*, in a less touristy village on the far side of the Danube, serves up award-winning wines with broccoli soufflé and ham noodles.

✉ Stammersdorfer Strasse 21, Stammersdorf ☎ 292 1684
🚌 31

## Zum Kuchldragoner (££)

Candlelit tavern-restaurant with terrace at the heart of the 'Bermuda Triangle'. Serves a range of traditional Austrian dishes.

✉ Ruprechtsplatz 4–5
☎ 533 8371 🚇 Swedenplatz

## Zum Kuckuck (£££)

Posh, but intimate restaurant in the traditional Viennese style with a large choice of Austrian dishes. Handy for St Stephen's Cathedral and other city sights.

✉ Himmelpfortgasse 15
☎ 512 8470 🕐 Closed Sun
🚇 Stephansplatz

### Première Café

While the house in which Mozart died has long since been demolished, Café Frauenhuber, just up the road, is still standing. In the 18th century the first floor was a concert hall belonging to the court caterer, Otto Jahn, and it was here in March 1791 that Mozart premièred his last piano concerto (K595). Six years later, Ludwig van Beethoven performed in the same hall.

# Eastern Austria

### Fresh fish
As Austria is without a coastline, the only fresh fish available comes from the numerous rivers and lakes. The most common are *Forellen* (trout), *Karpfen* (carp), *Zander* (pike perch) and *Fogosch* (perch), though you'll also find local varieties, like *Steckerl* from the Neusiedler See, usually barbecued with spices, but only available in summer.

## Baden
### Badner Stüberl (££)
Worth considering as many of Baden's restaurants are on the expensive side, this traditional pub serves a variety of Austrian standards.
✉ Gutenbrunnstrasse 19
🕐 Closed Tue

### Krainerhütte (£££)
This well-appointed restaurant is in a 19th-century country-style hotel on the edge of town. International and Austrian cooking.
✉ Helental ☎ 02252 445110

## Bruck an der Leitha
### Ungarische Krone (££–£££)
The 'Hungarian Crown' is a country-style inn, founded in 1726. Excellent cooking and first class wines.
✉ Parndorfer Strasse 1
☎ 02162 62777

## Dürnstein
### Loibnerhof (££)
Tasty food and good wine in a romantic setting. Packed at weekends in the apricot blossom season.
✉ Unterloiben 7 ☎ 02711
82890 🕐 Closed Mon, Tue

## Eisenstadt
### Café Esterházy (£££)
Located in the former stables of the castle, this chic eatery caters mainly for the theatre supper set. The bar stays open late, a point well worth remembering in this otherwise quiet town.
✉ Esterházyplatz 5 ☎ 02682
61505

### Haydnbräu (££)
Modern restaurant serving a typical range of Austrian dishes including fish; not forgetting the excellent local beer, brewed here since 1990.
✉ Pfarrgasse 22 ☎ 02682
61561

### Zum Eder (£–££)
Restaurant in the town centre offering a range of well-conceived and -presented dishes including salads and vegetable lasagne.
✉ Hauptstrasse 25 ☎ 02682
62645

## Graz
### Gambrinuskeller (££)
This inner town restaurant serves Balkan specialities including *Bohnensuppe* (bean soup), as well as Croatian and local wines and beers. Children's menu.
✉ Färbergasse 6-8 ☎ 0316
810181

### Glockenspiel (£)
An ideal place to stop for a coffee and a sandwich (or pastry) while waiting for the musical clock to go through its paces.
✉ Glockenspielplatz 4
🕐 Closed Sun

### Glockenspielkeller (££)
Good value Styrian dishes in handy, central location . You'll need the English language menu. Some outdoor seating.
✉ Mehlplatz 3 ☎ 0316
828701

### Landhauskeller (£££)
Wonderful setting in the courtyard of the historic Landhaus building. Styrian specialities.
✉ Schmiedgasse 9 ☎ 0316
830276 🕐 Closed Sun

### Mangolds (£)
Self-service vegetarian

restaurant with a good selection of healthy dishes. No credit cards.

✉ **Griesgasse 11** ☎ **0316 918002** 🕐 **Until 8PM Mon–Fri. Closed Sat PM, Sun**

### Schlossberg (£)
Terrace café with panoramic views of the city. The speciality of the house is *Germknödeln* (poppy seed dumplings).

✉ **Schlossberg** ☎ **0316 823050**

## Krems an der Donau
### Alte Post (£–££)
Appealing house, with a delightful Renaissance courtyard, located in the centre of Krems. Traditional Austrian dishes. No credit cards.

✉ **Obere Landstrasse 32** ☎ **02732 822760** 🕐 **Closed Jan–mid Mar**

## Mariazell
### Gasthof zum Jägerwirt (££)
*Schnitzels*, goulash dishes and other Austrian standards; also snacks and salads. No credit cards.

✉ **Hauptplatz 2** ☎ **03882 2362** 🕐 **Closed Mon**

### Goldener Ochs (££)
Popular family restaurant well worth trying for its grill specialities and friendly atmosphere. Terrace seating available in summer.

✉ **A. Krupp-Platz 3** ☎ **03882 2407** 🕐 **Closed Tue**

### Zum alten Brauhaus (£)
Styrian specialities washed down, ideally, by the excellent local Girrer brew, available on tap (ask for *Bier vom Fass*).

✉ **Wienerstrasse 5** ☎ **03882 25230**

## Neusiedler See
### Martinschenke (££)
A folksy thatched restaurant and grillhouse with garden and candlelit interior. Serves standard Austrian fare with fresh salads and a good selection of local wines.

✉ **Bodenzeile 14-16, Purbach** ☎ **02683 5151** 🕐 **Closed Wed**

### Nikolauszeche (£££)
Dining in this top-notch village restaurant will set you back a bit, but it's worth it both for the setting in a 15th-century house and for the superb regional cuisine. The more exotic specialities include pink fillet of young goat and the wines are from the Nikolauszeche cellars.

✉ **Bodenzeile, Purbach** ☎ **02683 5514**

### Schandl (£–££)
Plain home cooking is what's on offer in this typical Neusiedler See inn (*Buschenschank*). There's an attractive courtyard and the wines are good too. No credit cards.

✉ **Hauptstrasse 20, Rust** ☎ **02685 265** 🕐 **Closed Tue and Nov–Mar**

### Seewirt (££)
The restaurant in this waterfront hotel is good for local dishes, including fish. No credit cards.

✉ **Strandplatz 1, Podersdorf** ☎ **02177 2415**

### Zum Tabormandl (££)
A popular high street restaurant offering a wide range of pizza dishes as well as Austrian standards.

✉ **Obere Hauptstrasse 13, Neusiedl am See** ☎ **02167 2504**

### Prost! (Cheers!)
One of Burgenland's most distinguished wine producers is Schloss Esterházy in Eisenstadt with 50 hectares of vineyards, west of Neusiedler See and on the slopes of the Leitha mountains. You'll find their wines in restaurants all over the region. Esterházy specialises in the Burgunder grape, turning out delicate *Ruländer* (Pinot gris) and equally sensitive chardonnays. The castle cellars are open to the public for tours, after which you can stock up in the Vinothek.

# Central Austria

**Sprechen Sie Styrisch?**
A knowledge of Styrian dialect comes in handy when ordering in restaurants in the region. Some examples: *Oa* - German Ei (egg); *Fog* - German Schwein (pork); *Braten* – German Brot (bread); *Zwifl* – German Zwiebel (onion); *Knofl* – German Knoblauch (garlic); *soss* – German Sauce (sauce); *greste* – German *geröstet* (roasted); *tringan* – German *trinken* (to drink), *zoahln* – German bezahlen (to pay).

## Bad Ischl
### Café Zauner (££)
Bad Ischl's best known café, Zauner is famous for its desserts – try the *Zaunerstollen* (type of fruitcake).
Pfarrgasse 7 ☎ 06132 23522 ⏰ Lunch, dinner. Closed Tue

### Villa Schratt (£££)
The former home of Emperor Franz-Josef's mistress, Katharina Schratt, specialises in fish dishes.
Steinbruch 43 ☎ 06132 27647

## Freistadt
### Zum Goldenen Adler (£–££)
In the hotel of the same name, this restaurant is known for its regional specialities. Try the *Böhmisches bierfleisch* (beef cooked in beer), made with the local beer, Freistädter.
Salzgasse 1 ☎ 07942 721120

## Gmunden
### Lambi Mambi (££)
This traditional Gasthaus, serving imaginative Austrian cuisine, is a real find. No credit cards.
Linzer Strasse 37 ☎ 07612 67488 ⏰ Dinner only. Closed Sun

## Hallstatt
### Berggasthof Rudolfsturm (£££)
En route to the salt mines (2 mins from the cable car stop), this restaurant serves regional specialities and has a terrace with panoramic views.
Salzberg 1 ☎ 06134 8253

### Derbl (£)
Pleasant, if busy, café in the central square. Good on pizzas, better on desserts.
Markt 61 ☎ 06134 240

## Klagenfurt
### Molly Malone (£)
This lively Irish pub serves up decent helpings of chicken salad, fish and chips, Irish stew etc. Dependable late night atmosphere at weekends when closing time extends to the small hours.
Theatergasse 7 ☎ 0463 57200

### Seerestaurant Lido (££)
Stylish café and bistro with a beer garden overlooking the Wörther See, where you can relax with a *torte* or an ice cream until the boat comes in.
Am Friedelstrand 1 ☎ 0463 242344

### Zum Augustin (££)
Noisy, crowded beer bar near the Pfarrkirche with plenty of atmosphere. Carinthian noodle dishes are the speciality of the house, but you'll need to grab a table early.
Pfarrhofgasse 2 ☎ 0463 513992 ⏰ Closed Sun

## Salzburg
### Andreas Hofer (£–££)
This wine bar and restaurant has a warm welcoming atmosphere with candlelit rooms and friendly service. Tirolean specialities, including gröstel (pan-fried potatoes, pork, onions and spices) and good fresh salads. Reservations recommended.
Steingasse 65 ☎ 0662 872769

### Bella Vita (££–£££)
The full range of Italian cuisine is on offer in this

popular restaurant a little way from the town centre.

✉ **Vogelweiderstrasse 9**
☎ 0662 883338 🕐 **Closed Sun**

### Café-Hartl (£)

Moderately-priced créperie (also pizzas) with branches on both sides of the river.

✉ **Kaigasse 13/Linzergasse 23**
☎ 0662 846867/878284

### Gasthof Krimpelstätter (££)

Dine in the atmospheric surroundings of a 16th-century inn, not far from the old town. Standard Austrian cuisine and Augustiner beer on tap. Beer garden.

✉ **Müllner Hauptstrasse 31**
☎ 0662 432274

### Stiftskeller St Peter (££)

The former monastic refectory, dates from AD 803, making this the oldest restaurant in central Europe. (According to local tradition Mephistopheles met Faust here.) Poached fish is one of the specialities.

✉ **Stiftsbezirk 1–4** ☎ 0662 841268-0

### Weisses Kreuz (£)

Excellent Balkan specialities, including spicy fillet steak, courgette soup, and rice with pork and paprika. Those with an appetite can try the Balkan Platter, consisting of five different dishes.

✉ **Bierjodlgasse 6** ☎ 0662 845641 🕐 **Closed Tue (except Jul & Aug)**

### Winkler (££)

Terraced restaurant on the Mönchsberg with wonderful views over the town. Ideal for lunch or morning coffee.

✉ **Am Mönchsberg** ☎ 0662 847738 🕐 **Closed Mon**

### Zum Eulenspiegel (£££)

Reservations are essential at this characterful restaurant opposite Mozart's birthplace. Ask the English-speaking staff to steer you through the Austrian specialities; also good fish.

✉ **Hagenauerplatz 2** ☎ 0662 843180 🕐 **Closed Sun**

## Steyr
### Zu den Drei Rosen (£–££)

Pleasant restaurant with outdoor dining and very reasonable prices in the Mader Hotel, right in the centre of town. The set menu is particularly good value.

✉ **Stadtplatz 36** ☎ 07252 533580 🕐 **Closed Sun**

## Wörther See
### Landskron (£££)

Dine out within the precincts of this 16th-century hilltop castle not far from Villach. Medieval six-course dinners on Tuesday nights (with serving wenches!).

✉ **Burgruine, Landskron** ☎ 04242 41563

### Primus Haus (££)

Friendly café-restaurant two minutes' walk from the landing stage. Pizzas, standard Austrian dishes and Balkan *Cevapcici* (meatballs in tomato sauce).

✉ **Maria Wörth** ☎ 04273 2500

### Rainer's (£££)

Excellent restaurant with views from balcony tables. Some of the tables have balcony views.

✉ **Monte-Carlo-Platz 1, Pörtschach** ☎ 04272 2300 🕐 **Dinner. Closed mid Sep–mid May**

### The World of Beer

Brewery visits are a speciality of the Salzburg region. Stiegl, Austria's biggest private brewery and Salzburg's oldest with a tradition dating back to 1492, has its own museum with entertaining demonstrations of the various beer making processes, including a section on bottled beers. There are tastings and you can even try creating your own personal brew.

✉ **Bräuhausstrasse 9** ☎ 0662 8387 115

# Western Austria

## Tirolean Evening

If you're staying in the Tirol, why not let your hair down and head off to a Tirolean Evening. Here you'll see singers and dancers in traditional costumes performing the famous *Schuhplatter* (clog dance) as well as yodelling and brass band music. As a taster, watch one of the performances that take place occasionally outside the Goldenes Dachl in Innsbruck (➤ 82). (Contact tourist information office for details.)

## Arlberg

### Jägerstube (££)

The restaurant belongs to the noted skier, Karl Schranz, and is part of a hotel accessed from the town by bus. No credit cards.

☒ St Anton ☎ 05446 25550
◉ Closed May–Jun, Oct–Nov

### Krone (£££)

Upmarket hotel-restaurant for gourmets who enjoy game and fish specialities. No credit cards.

☒ Haus 13 (between the river and the church), Lech
☎ 05583 2551

### Pizzeria la Taverna (£)

Good selection of pizza toppings, pasta dishes etc.

☒ Vorstadt 20, Feldkirch
☎ 05522 79293

### Schäfle (£££)

Expensive, but this traditional restaurant has a *gemütlich* (genial) ambience and good regional dishes with interesting sauces.

☒ Naflastrasse 3, Feldkirch
☎ 05522 722030 ◉ Closed Sun

## Bregenz

### Deuringschlössle (£££)

Reservations are essential in this smart restaurant in a 400 year old castle. Austrian and international dishes are prepared to perfection.

☒ Ehregutplatz 4 ☎ 05574 47800

### Goldener Hirschen (£)

Old town inn, with a busy, convivial atmosphere. Go for the pasta dishes.

☒ Kirchstrasse 8 ☎ 05574 42815 ◉ Closed Tues and part of Sep

## Innsbruck

### Ottoburg (£–££)

Busy restaurant in a late 15th-century house near the river Inn. Upstairs is more exclusive but the choice of Austrian dishes is a little less predictable than downstairs.

☒ Herzog-Friedrich-Strasse 1
☎ 0512 574652 ◉ Closed Tue

### Philippine (£)

Excellent range of vegetarian dishes and a nice relaxed atmosphere. None of the dishes are expensive, but best value is the *Tagesmenü* (menu of the day).

☒ Müllerstrasse 9 ☎ 0512 589157 ◉ Closed Sun

### Schwarzer Adler (££)

Comfortable establishment serving typical Austrian cuisine, with the added bonus of a good view towards the Old Town.

☒ Kaiserjägerstrasse 2
☎ 0512 587109

### Seegrube (£££)

Travel by funicular, then cable-car, to dine at 1,400m on the Nordkette with Innsbruck spread out at your feet and the central Alps all around – breathtaking!

☒ Nordkette ☎ 0512 290520
◉ Cable-car at half-hourly intervals until 23:30

### Stiftskeller (££)

Located in a quaint alleyway near the Hofburg, this popular restaurant serves a variety of Austrian and fish dishes.

☒ Stiftgasse 1 ☎ 0512 583490

### Sweet Basil (££)

Trendy late-night bar and restaurant on several levels,

in the heart of the old town.

✉ **Herzog-Friedrich Strasse 31**
☎ **0512 584996** ⏰ **Until 1AM (2AM Thu–Sat)**

### Thai-Li (£££)
Excellent Thai food is served in this popular restaurant in the old town. Booking essential.

✉ **Marktgraben 3** ☎ **0512 562813**

### Tiroler Stuben (£££)
This restaurant, on the edge of the Old Town, is in great demand because of its range of Tirolean specialities, including *Schlutzkrapferln* (ravioli).

✉ **Innrain 13** ☎ **0512 577931**

## Kitzbühel
### Chizzo (£)
Good value Tirolean food served in pleasant surroundings, including outdoor terrace.

✉ **Josef-Herold-Strasse 2**
☎ **053566 2475**

### Tennerhof (£££)
Exclusive (and very expensive) Tirolean restaurant famous throughout the region for the standard of its cooking. Jacket and tie essential and you'll need to book a table.

✉ **Griesenauweg 26**
☎ **053566 3181** ⏰ **Closed Apr–mid-May, mid-Oct–mid-Dec**

## Kufstein
### Hotel Zum Bären (£££)
Excellent restaurant housed in a 17th-century hotel. The cuisine focuses on Tyrolian specialities and has been awarded the coveted 'Tiroler Wirtshaus' cachet.

✉ **Salurnerstrasse 36**
☎ **05372 63689-4**

## Ötztal
### Goldenes Fassl (££)
Handy eaterie en route to the mountains, serving the usual Tirolean and Austrian dishes

✉ **Malsergasse, Landeck**
☎ **664 356 1839**

## Zell am See
### Café Feinschmeck (££)
This welcoming café-restaurant is part of a new hotel in the pedestrianised town centre. Austrian standards including turkey *Schnitzel* (cutlet fried in breadcrumbs) and there's a non-smoking section.

✉ **Dreifaltigkeitsgasse 10**
☎ **06542 72549**

### Schloss Prielau (£££)
As the name suggests, a castle setting for this elegant restaurant presenting mainstream Austrian cuisine with flair and imagination.

✉ **Hofmannsthalstrasse**
☎ **06542 2609**

### Zum Hirschen (££)
Dine in typical Austrian wood-panelled surroundings on light dishes and regional specialities. Comfortable and relaxed.

✉ **Dreifaltigkeitsgasse 1**
☎ **06542 2447**

## Zillertal
### Kramerwirt (£££)
An excellent venue for trying out quality Tirolean cuisine. No credit cards.

✉ **Am Marienbrunnen 346, Mayrhofen** ☎ **05285 6700**

### Zillerhof (££)
Popular pizzeria in the hotel of the same name.

✉ **Banhofstrasse 3, Zell am Ziller** ☎ **05282 2610**
⏰ **Closed mid-Oct–mid-Jun**

### Coffee Delights
The coffee house is a way of life in Austria and some Viennese establishments offer as many as 40 versions of the national drink, invariably served up with a glass of water. A favourite with many Austrians is the *Melange* (half coffee, half frothy milk – pronounced as in French). Ask for a *kleine Braune* and you'll get a black coffee with a dash of cream. If you're feeling more adventurous, try an *Einspänner* – black coffee with whipped cream (*Schlagobers*), served in a glass. Or, if you really want to go over the top, demand a *Maria Theresa*, a large glass of black coffee laced with orange and mocca liqueur and surmounted by a dob of whipped cream and a sprinkling of chocolate.

99

# Vienna

## Prices
For two people in a double room with breakfast.
£ = AS 600–1,500
££ = AS 1,500–2,500
£££ = AS 2,500+

## Hotel Sacher
One of Vienna's most venerable hotels is Sacher, famous for its café and *Sachertorte*. It was founded in 1876 and run for many years by the cigar-smoking Anna Sacher, a formidable character who in 1919 prevented a working-class mob from invading the premises. Some scenes from the film *The Third Man* were shot in the lobby in 1949 and the director, Carol Reed, complimented the barman on the quality of his Bloody Marys.

## Hotel Am Schubertring (£££)
Small, comfortable hotel with convenient location, handy for shopping and sightseeing in the old town.
✉ Schubertring 11 ☎ 717 020, fax 713 9966 🚇 Stadtpark

## Hotel Praterstern (£)
The plain but comfortable rooms in this characterful hotel are equipped with shower and toilet.
✉ Mayergasse 6 ☎ 214 0123, fax 214 7880 🚇 Nestroyplatz

## Hotel Sacher (£££)
The celebrated Sachertorte (chocolate cake) takes its name from the café in this luxury hotel which dates from the 19th century (▶ panel).
✉ Philharmonikerstrasse 4 ☎ 514 560, fax 514 56810 🚇 Oper

## Kärntnerhof (££–£££)
This quietly situated hotel, not far from St Stephen's Cathedral, has large bedrooms and friendly staff.
✉ Grashofgasse 4 ☎ 512 1923, fax 513 2228 🚇 Schwedenplatz

## Kolbeck 'Zur Linde' (£)
Conveniently situated for the Südbahnhof, with 24-hour reception.
✉ Laxenburger Strasse 19 ☎ 604 1773, fax 604 9486

## König von Ungarn (£££)
This beautifully modernised hotel, virtually on top of St Stephen's, is actually a 16th-century house – the old courtyard has been preserved.
✉ Schulerstrasse 10 ☎ and fax 515 8400 🚇 Stephansplatz

## Palais Schwarzenberg (£££)
This luxury hotel, standing in its own park, occupies one of the best locations in the city.
✉ Schwarzenbergplatz 9 ☎ 798 4515. fax 798 4714 🚇 Karlsplatz

## Pension City (££)
Friendly hotel with central location in an elegant turn-of-the-century building.
✉ Bauernmarkt 10 ☎ 533 9521, fax 535 5216 🚇 Stephansplatz

## Pension Falstaff (£)
Respected pension with 'no frills' rooms in a 19th-century building.
✉ Müllnergasse 5 ☎ 317 9127, fax 3127 9186 🚇 D 🚇 Rossauer-Lände

## Pension Lerner (££)
Plain comfortable rooms with shower and satellite TV. The hearty breakfast is a plus.
✉ Wipplingerstrasse 23 ☎ 533 5219, fax 533 5678 🚇 Schottentor/Herrengasse

## Pension Pertschy (££–£££)
Ideally situated near the Graben, the rooms in this former town house are modern and a good size.
✉ Habsburgergasse 5 ☎ 534 490, fax 534 4949 🚇 Stephensplatz

## Pension Riedl (££)
Pleasant pension in an atmospheric *fin de siècle* building. Although the rooms are small, they have toilet and shower en suite and you can have breakfast in bed!
✉ Georg-Coch-Platz 3 ☎ and fax 512 7919 🚇 Schwedenplatz/Wien-Mitte

# Eastern Austria

## Baden

### Grand Hotel Sauerhof (£££)

Stylish, luxury hotel in a former palace. Facilities include indoor swimming pool, sauna and tennis court.

✉ Weilburgstrasse 11–13
☎ 02252 41251, fax 02252 48047

## Dürnstein

### Pension Altes Rathaus (£)

Characterful sgraffitoed building, dating from the 16th century. Good location.

✉ Hauptstrasse 26 ☎ 02711 252

### Schloss Hotel Dürnstein (£££)

This luxury hotel, with indoor and outdoor swimming pools and sauna, occupies a 17th-century castle. Magnificent views of the Danube – you can dine out overlooking the river.

✉ Dürnstein ☎ 02711 212, fax 02711 351

## Eisenstadt

### Gasthof Familie Ohr (££)

Quiet, comfortable rooms and an excellent restaurant (closed Mon) are the main attractions of this medium-sized hotel, situated between the station and the town.

✉ Rusterstrasse 51
☎ 02682 62460, fax 02682 624609

## Graz

### Hotel Drei Raben (££)

Modern hotel on a busy street with tram routes. Comfortable and surprisingly quiet given the location.

✉ Annenstrasse 43 ☎ 0316 712686, fax 0316 7159596

### Hotel Pfeifer 'Zum Kirchenwirt' (£££)

A few kilometres northeast of Graz, this 300-year old hotel has a rural feel and the beer garden has a delightful view of the city.

✉ Kirchplatz 9 ☎ 0316 391112, fax 0316 39111249

### Schlossberg Hotel (£££)

Elegantly furnished hotel with an ideal location between the Schlossberg and the main square. Facilities include sauna, solarium, fitness room and a rooftop swimming pool with garden. Underground car park.

✉ Kaiser-Franz-Josef-Kai 30 ☎ 0316 3168070, fax 0316 316807070

## Krems

### Hotel Unter den Linden (££)

Pleasant, quietly situated inn with garden. Cheaper rooms are available, if you don't mind sharing a bathroom.

✉ Schillerstrasse 5
☎ 02732 82115, fax 02732 82115-20

## Neusiedler See

### Romantik-Purbachhof (££)

This beautifully restored wine-grower's house, dating from the 16th century, is an absolute delight with simply furnished, characterful rooms and a sunny courtyard for lingering breakfasts.

✉ Schulgasse 14, Purbach ☎ and fax 02683 5564

### Rusterhof (£££)

Former Burgherhaus in the centre of this delightful little town with rooms and apartments. The restaurant is also worth investigating.

✉ Rathausplatz 18, Rust ☎ 02685 6416 🕐 Closed Jan–Apr

### Hotels with Character

If you're in the mood and can afford to treat yourself, look out for the Romantik and Schloss Hotel chains. Not only can you expect high quality accommodation, but you'll be staying in a building with a bit of history or character. Many Austrian hotels are converted castles, monasteries, palaces or villas built by 19th-century industrialists in scenic locations. The rooms in these establishments are correspondingly spacious and invariably tastefully furnished, often with antiques.

# Central Austria

**Spoilt for Choice**

If you don't want to stay in a hotel, there are plenty of other choices available. A *Pension* or *Hotel Garni* offers bed and breakfast only, while a *Gasthaus/Gästehaus* is a rustic inn, usually with just a few rooms available. Like many smaller hotels in Austria, these are often family-run with a homely atmosphere. You may be expected to stay for at least a few days – one inducement to do so is to charge more for the first night.

## Bad Ischl
### Zum Goldenen Schiff (££–£££)
Medium-sized hotel where some of the balconied rooms look out onto the river. Fish restaurant.
✉ Adalbert-Stiftter-Kai 3 ☎ 06132 24241, fax 06132 2424156

## Gmunden
### Goldener Brunnen (££)
Comfortable rooms in the town centre with en suite facilities.
✉ Traungasse 10 ☎ 07612 4431, fax 07612 443255

## Halstatt
### Bräugasthof Halstatt
Already on the map in 1472, this large hotel with comfortable rooms overlooks the lake. Terrace restaurant offering fish specialities.
✉ Seestrasse 120 ☎ 06134 8221

## Klagenfurt
### Hotel Liebetegger (£–££)
Friendly, homely and quiet, this unassuming family-run hotel is not too far from the town centre. Unexceptional rooms, but excellent breakfast.
✉ Völkermarkterstrasse 8 ☎ 056935, fax 056835

## Salzburg
### Goldener Hirsch (£££)
Mozart himself may have been familiar with 'The Golden Stag', a venerable building dating from around 1400. Sensitively furnished rooms. (Extra charge for breakfast.)
✉ Getreidegasse 37 ☎ 0662 8084, fax 0662 848511

### Hotel Goldene Krone (££)
Friendly, family-run hotel on the right bank, convenient for sightseeing but rather noisy. There are cheaper rooms without en suite facilities. It might be worth opting for breakfast in town. No credit cards.
✉ Linzer Gasse 48 ☎ 0662 8723

### Weisse Taube (££)
This family-run hotel is an adapted 14th-century building with some quaint features, though the rooms are nothing special.
✉ Kaigasse 9 ☎ 0662 842404, fax 0662 841783

## Wörther See
### Hubertushof (££–£££)
A pair of converted turn-of-the-century villas overlooking the lake with indoor swimming pool and sauna.
✉ Europaplatz 1, Velden ☎ 04274 2676, fax 04274 265760

### Schloss Halleg (£–££)
A converted 13th-century castle in a quiet, but accessible Wörther See resort. The rooms are comfortable and although there's no restaurant, there are plenty within reach as well as a lake for that early morning swim. No credit cards.
✉ Hallegger Strasse 131, Krumpendorf ☎ 0463 49311

### Schloss Leonstein (££)
Surprisingly homely, considering that this hotel is a converted medieval castle. One drawback is the traffic noise; on the other hand the facilities, including tennis, golf and boating, are excellent.
✉ Hauptstrasse 228 ☎ 04272 28160, fax 04272 2823

# Western Austria

## Arlberg
### Gasthof Post (££–£££)
The excellent restaurant is the main draw at this charming, chalet-style hotel. Indoor pool and sauna. The hotel doesn't accept credit cards.

✉ **Dorf-11, Lech** ☎ **05583 22060, fax 05583 220623** 🕐 **Closed mid-Apr to Jun, mid-Sep to Nov**

## Bregenz
### Hotel Bodensee (££)
All rooms in this medium-priced hotel have TV and en suite facilities. The breakfast is good value.

✉ **Kornmarktstrasse 22** ☎ **05574 423000, fax 05574 45168**

## Innsbruck
### Goldener Adler (£££)
Innsbruck's most famous hotel, in a beautiful medieval street, has played host to royalty and celebrities, most notably Mozart and Goethe. Most of the rooms are spacious and there are two quality restaurants.

✉ **Herzog-Friedrich-Strasse 6** ☎ **0512 586334, fax 0512 584409**

### Hotel-Gasthof Bierwirt (£££)
Classy hotel-pension in chalet-type building. Restaurant offering Tirolean specialities.

✉ **Bichlweg 2** ☎ **0512 342143, fax 0512 3421435**

### Hotel Royal (££)
Don't be put off by the uninspired exterior, the rooms in this conveniently situated hotel are large and comfortable.

✉ **Innrain 16** ☎ **0512 586385, fax 0512 58638510**

## Kitzbühel
### Hörl (£)
On the way to the railway station, this good-value budget hotel has single and double rooms, some of which have en suite facilities.

✉ **Josef-Pirchler-Strasse 60** ☎ **and fax 05356 3144**

### Weisses Rössl (££)
Welcoming, centrally located hotel with pine-decorated rooms, restaurant, bars and tennis court.

✉ **Bichlstrasse 3–5** ☎ **05356 62541, fax 05356 63472** 🕐 **Closed mid-Apr to mid-May, mid-Oct to early Dec**

## Zell am See
### Gasthof Schmittental (££)
Chalet-hotel, just a little to the west of the town centre. All rooms have en suite facilities and TV.

✉ **Schmittenstrasse 60** ☎ **and fax 06542 72332**

### Hotel Krimmlerfälle (£££)
Pleasant chalet-style hotel near the famous Krimml falls. Facilities include restaurant, indoor and outdoor swimming pools, sauna, solarium and fitness suite.

✉ **Wasserfallstrasse 42, Krimml** ☎ **06564 7203, fax 06564 7473**

## Zillertal
### Kramerwirt (££)
Completely refurbished 17th-century hotel, bustling with activity. The rooms are comfortable and there's a sauna as well as a restaurant and bar. No credit cards

✉ **Am Marienbrunnen 346, Mayrhofen** ☎ **05285 6700, fax 05285 670052** 🕐 **Closed part Dec**

## Tourism
Austria currently receives more than 17 million visitors from abroad anually, well over twice the total population. More than 78,000 establishments with a total of 1.2 million beds cater for overnight stays. The Tirol, Salzburg and Carinthia are the most popular tourist destinations, while the largest number of visitors come from Germany, the Netherlands and Switzerland.

# Supermarkets & Foodstores

### Confectioner
It was in 1890 that Salzburg confectioner, Paul Fürst, first dreamed up *Mozartkugeln*. These delicious balls of marzipan, rolled in nougat cream, then dipped in bittersweet chocolate, are still made by Konditorei Fürst, though no longer by hand. No one has yet been able to come up with a specific Mozart connection, although the great man did have a sweet tooth.

## Graz
### Hofbäckerei Edegger-Tax
Once the imperial bakery – hence the splendid carved crest above the doorway – this building dates from 1569. As well as the bakery, there's a small café where you can sample *Hofkaffée*, the speciality of the house – a coffee with egg liqueur, whipped cream and chocolate.
✉ Hofgasse 6 ☎ 0316 830230

## Innsbruck
### Spezialitäten aus der Stiftgasse
Visit this vaulted cellar to shop for quality Austrian wines and brandies.
✉ Stiftgasse 2 🕐 Mon–Fri 9:30–6:30

## Salzburg
### Julius Meinl
Branch of the famous Austrian supermarket chain, with wines, delicatessen counter etc.
✉ Griesgasse 19 🕐 Closed Sun

### Tee and Co.
More than 100 exotic and classic teas from around the world.
✉ Griesgasse 7 ☎ 0662 844 644

## Vienna
### Anker
Bakery chain selling cakes and pastries as well as fresh bread. Most branches have a snack counter and you can sometimes buy breakfast.
✉ Stock-im-Eisen-Platz; Bräuner Strasse etc.
🕐 Mon–Sat 8–12:30

### Anzinger
Purveyor of traditional Viennese chocolate specialities including *Mozartkugeln* (► panel). This branch is off Kärtner Strasse, there's another on Albertinaplatz.
✉ Tegetthoffstrasse 7
☎ 513 6553

### Billa
Austrian supermarket chain, just across the road from Schloss Belvedere.
✉ Rennweg 9

### Confiserie Walter Heindl
Purveyors of the famous *Mozartkugeln* chocolates as well as other delights including *Sissi Taler* (made from apricot-marzipan and chocolate cream).
✉ Rotenturmstrasse 16 (corner of Fleischmarkt)
☎ 667 2110

### Demmers Teehaus
Although Vienna is more famous for its coffee, there's no shortage of customers at this popular tea shop. There's a salon upstairs where you can imbibe.
✉ Mölker Bastei 5 ☎ 535 5995 🕐 Mon–Wed, Fri 9–6:30, Thu 9–8, Sat 9–12:30

### Julius Meinl
Downtown supermarket with an excellent delicatessen counter and lunch area.
✉ Graben 19 ☎ 533 4586
🕐 Closed Sat 12:30, Sun

### Vinothek Bei Per Piaristenkirche
The place to buy Austrian wines including *Grüner Veltliner*, *Weissburgunder* and *Riesling*.
✉ Piaristengasse 54 ☎ 405 9553 🕐 Mon–Fri 2:30–6, Sat 9–12

# Souvenir Shops

## Graz

### Steirisches Heimatwerk

For an evocative souvenir of your stay in Styria, head for this handicraft shop where you'll find everything from dolls with embroidered costumes to folk outfits, inscribed glassware and tankards, porcelain and ornaments. This branch is next door to the Landthaus, there's another on Paulustorgasse.

✉ **Herrengasse 10** ☎ **0316 829045**

## Gmunden

### Gmundner Keramik

First produced in the 16th century, Gmunden pottery is famous for its distinctive green swirls and curlicues on a white base.

✉ **Keramikstrasse 24**
☎ **07612 54410**

## Hallstatt

### Keramik Hallstatt

Waterfront shop selling an excellent range of handmade, painted and decorated ceramics.

✉ **Wolfengasse 107**
☎ **06134 8460**

## Innsbruck

### Joh Wilhelm Heimtextil

Smart shop selling hand-produced traditional Tirolean embroidery and brocade – table linen, chair runners, aprons etc.

✉ **Maria-Theresien-Strasse 2**
☎ **0512 581171**

## Vienna

### Augarten

Manufacturers of Viennese porcelain since 1718, there are occasional thematic exhibitions in the store.

✉ **Graben/Stock-Im-Eisen-Platz** ☎ **512 1494**

### K+K Domgasse

Just down the street from the Mozart House, so it's not surprising that there's a shop specialising in Mozart memorabilia.

✉ **Domgasse 2** ☎ **512 6167**

### Lobmeyr

Founded in 1823, this is one of Austria's most famous purveyors of glassware, specialising in crystal chandeliers. Also sells porcelain and silverware – the shopfront is eye-catching too.

✉ **Kärntnerstrasse 26**
☎ **512 0508** 🕑 **Closed Sat PM, Sun**

### Pawlata

This upmarket outlet specialises in rustic ceramics from the Gmunden region.

✉ **Kärntnerstrasse 14**
☎ **512 1764**

### Schloss Schönbrunn Museum Shop

Novelty watches, books, cards, CDs, videos and other themed merchandise.

✉ **Schönbrunner Schlossstrasse 47** ☎ **512 81113**

### Trachten Tostmann

Store specialising in Austrian handicrafts and costumes, located just up the road from the Burgtheater.

✉ **Schottengasse 3a** ☎ **533 5331**

## Zell am See

### Anna Frank

Swarowski silver crystal and other glassware and ceramic items are on sale in this local shop. There's also a branch in the Vogtturm.

✉ **Seegasse 9** ☎ **06542 72574**

### Gifts

Glass, ceramics and pottery make dependable gifts, although they don't necessarily come cheap. Look out for brightly painted Gmundner ceramics or Augarten porcelain. Austria is famous for its crystal. Lobmeyr glassware of Vienna is world reknowned, but alternatives are Riedel in Jenbach and Swarowski which has an enormous warehouse in Wattens, just outside Innsbruck. Other ideas include embroidered table linen, sweets and chocolate, pumpkinseed oil (*Kürbisnöl*) and of course Austrian wine.

# Clothes Shops &
# Department Stores

**Historic shop**
The arcaded building known as Paradeishof, and now occupied by the Kastner & Öhler department store, has a fascinating history. In the 15th century it was owned by the aristocratic Eggenberg family. During the Reformation, when it became the Protestant cathedral school, the astronomer Johannes Kepler was on the staff. He fled to Prague when the Catholics returned, handing the building over to the monastic Order of Poor Clares. One of the later residents was a minor composer, Wilhelm Kienzl-Evangelimann.

## Graz

### Kastner & Öhler
Huge glass-fronted department store selling everything from children's toys to Austrian folk music, CDs and videos, clothes etc.
 ✉ **Sackstrasse 7–13**
☎ **0316 8703643**

## Innsbruck

### Sportler Witting
A wide range of sports clothes and equipment is displayed over six floors in this city centre store.
✉ **Maria-Theresien-Strasse 39** ☎ **0512 589144**

### Textilhaus Egger
Traditional woollen jackets and folk costumes for men and women. Also table and bed linen.
✉ **Herzog-Friedrich-Strasse 15**

## Linz

### Arkade
Busy shopping mall on a pedestrianised street in the town centre. Shops include Ö Heimatwerk, selling ceramics, fabrics, silverware etc.
✉ **Landstrasse**

## Salzburg

### Dschulnigg
The best place to shop for the traditional Austrian folk costume – lederhosen, dirndls etc.
✉ **Griesgasse 8** ☎ **0662 842376**

### Stassny Trachtenkinder
Fit out your kids in traditional Austrian dress – waistcoats, blouses, pinafores, lederhosen and hats, all in children's sizes.
✉ **Getreidegasse 30** ☎ **0662 842357**

## Vienna

### Chegini
Upmarket women's fashions of taste and style.
✉ **Kohlmarkt 7** ☎ **533 2058**
🕐 **Mon–Fri 9:45–6, Sat 10–1**

### Peek & Cloppenburg
The best known (but also the most expensive) of several fashion department stores on this busy shopping street. There are restaurants in the basement.
✉ **Mariahilferstrasse 26–30**
☎ **525 610**

### Ringstrassen Galerien
Large shopping complex in the heart of Vienna with 70 stores as well as restaurants and ample parking.
✉ **Kärntner Ring 5–7, 9–13**

### Taki-To Shop
Exclusive children's fashions by quality Austrian designers. Includes sports clothes and accessories.
✉ **Petersplatz 8** ☎ **535 1823**
🕐 **Mon–Fri 10–6, Sat 10:30–4:30**

### *Trachtenmoden* Shops
Outlets selling traditional clothing, including the Austrian national costume, can be found in various locations in central Vienna. Typical, and very handily situated for St Stephen's Cathedral, is **Witzky**
✉ **Stephansplatz 7 (near the horse and trap stop)** ☎ **512 4843**

## Wörther See

### Peter Tschebull
Shopping chain selling smart ladies and men's fashions and sportswear with branch in Villach.
✉ **Am Korso 23, Velden**
☎ **04274 2473**

# Other Shops

## Eisenstadt
### Haydnshop
Books, CDs and other momentoes of the famous composer are available here.
✉ **Schloss Esterházy**
☎ **02682 6338428**

## Graz
### Kunst Stücke
Craft and design shop, featuring work by local artist Viktoria Zöhrer-Vogt.
✉ **Sackstrasse 20 (by the castle steps)** ☎ **0316 821919**

### Steirisches Heimatwerk
These two outlets of Graz's folklore museum (at Paulustorgasse 13) display an appealing range of Styrian crafts. The Herrengasse branch has hand-crafted decorative items, clothes and silver jewellery, while the Paulustorgasse shop sells fabrics. If you are here in Advent visit the traditional Christmas market in the cellar of the folk museum.
✉ **Herrengasse 10, Paulustorgasse 4**

## Innsbruck
### Geigenbaumeister
The shop sells violin accessories but the real draw is local craftsman Wolfgang Kozák. You can watch him repairing old musical instruments and making new ones.
✉ **Universitätsstrasse 3–1**

### Lektüre
A large bookstore in the centre of town with a good selection of maps, guides etc.
✉ **Maria-Theresien-Strasse 16** ☎ **0512 580888**

### Swarowski
The famed crystal ware of Daniel Swarovski has now

been around for almost a century and has lost none of its fascination. You can buy glassware, jewellery and objects made of crystal – swans, candleholders, clocks, ships, keyrings etc. There are also regular glass-blowing displays.
✉ **Innstrasse 1, Wattens**
☎ **05224 5886** 🕐 **May–Sep, Mon–Sat 8–6, Sun 8–12; Oct–Apr Mon–Fri 8–6, Sat 8–12**

## Salzburg
### Fritz Kreis
Classy craft shop specialising in ceramics, glassware and woodcarved items.
✉ **Sigmund-Haffner-Gasse 14**
☎ **0662 841768**

### Trödlerstube
An Aladdin's cave of antiques.
✉ **Linzergasse 50** ☎ **0662 871453**

## Vienna
### Buchhandlung Tyrolia
Conveniently located just behind St Stephen's Cathedral, this large bookstore has a selection of English language glossy titles on Vienna and Austria as well as local maps and guides.
✉ **Stephansplatz 5** ☎ **512 4840** 🕐 **Closed Sat PM, Sun**

### EMI
Huge selection of CDs and cassettes, classical and pop; also videos.
✉ **Kärntnerstrasse 30**
☎ **512 3675**

### Spielzeugschachtel
Large store selling a wide range of wooden and hand-crafted toys.
✉ **Rauhensteingasse 5**
☎ **512 4494**

### *Trachten*
*Trachten*, the traditional Austrian costumes, are worn throughout Austria but especially in the Salzburger Land. For men it's *Lederhosen* (leather shorts), embroidered braces, socks and hunting caps; for women the *Dirndl* (gathered skirt), white linen blouses, *Loden* (woollen jackets) and silk scarves. If you ask at the local tourist office, they will be able to put you in touch with one of the small workshops where these costumes are tailor-made.

# Children's Activities

## Swimming

Although there is no sea in Austria the country's lakes and beaches are one large play area for children – if they enjoy watersports, so much the better. Most resorts also have supervised indoor and outdoor swimming pools, many of them heated.

## Theme Parks

### Märchenpark

This fairytale and leisure park will appeal to young children, with its ghost castle, monorail, baby animals for stroking, life-size fairy tale characters and fairground rides.

✉ **Am Rusterberg, St Margarethen, Neusiedler See** ☎ **02685 60707** 🕐 **Mar–Oct 9–6 (attractions 10–6)** 💷 **Moderate**

### Minimundus

The 'miniature world' is a park with scale models of some of the world's most famous monuments, some familiar, others less so. Convenient for play areas and other child-centred activities, swimming etc.

✉ **Villacher Strasse, Klagenfurt** ☎ **0463 21194-0** 🕐 **Mid–late-Apr, early–mid-Oct 9–5; May–Jun, Sep 9–6; Jul–Aug Sun–Tue, Thu–Fri 8–7, Wed, Sat 8AM–9PM**

### Play Castle Tirol

Designed on the lines of a medieval castle, this 12,000sq m theme park has everything from train sets and cuddly toys to computer games, state-of-the-art videos, virtual reality games, skating rinks, skateboarding ramps, climbing walls and a FunDome.

✉ **Am Schlossberg, Seefeld, nr Innsbruck** ☎ **05212 3737** 🕐 **Daily** 💷 **Moderate**

### Prater

All the fun of the fair with a huge choice of rides, side shows etc. (► 38)

✉ **Prater, Vienna** 🚇 **Praterstern** 💷 **Park free, pay for rides**

## Seegrotte

In the Hinterbrühl region of the Wienerwald (Vienna Woods), is Europe's largest underground lake grotto where boat trips explore the various galleries.

✉ **Hinterbrühl bei Wien** ☎ **02236 26364** 🕐 **9–5** 💷 **Expensive**

### Zwergenpark

Gnome garden with miniature railway.

✉ **Gurk, Carinthia** ☎ **04266 8077** 🕐 **May–Aug 9–6; Sep–mid-Oct 10–6** 💷 **Cheap**

## Zoos & Wildlife Parks

### Alpen Wildpark

A deer park with areas for petting animals, and wildlife exhibition.

✉ **Feld am See, Carinthia** ☎ **04246 2776** 🕐 **May–15 Oct** 💷 **Cheap**

### Alpenzoo

More than 2,000 Alpine animals roam this unusual zoo, spectacularly situated on the Hungerburg mountain above Innsbruck. Even access, via a cog railway, is enjoyable.

✉ **Weiherburggasse 37, Innsbruck** ☎ **0512 292323** 🕐 **Summer 9–6, winter 9–dusk** 💷 **Moderate**

### Safari-und-Abenteuer Park Gänserndorf

The park is a mixture of safari park with lions, tigers, antelopes, camels, zebras, giraffes, monkeys, sea lion shows etc and adventure park with acrobats, dare devil acts, trampolines and kiddy rides.

✉ **Sieben Brunnerstrasse, Gänserdorf, east of Vienna**

☎ 02282 702610 🕐 Apr–last Sun Oct 9:30–3 ✋ Moderate (all-inclusive)

## Mines

If you're in the Salzkammergut or the Innsbruck area, you should certainly consider taking the children on an excursion to one of the mines (► 18, 87). Not only do you learn about the workings, you get to travel underground on special mine trains, and there are other attractions like slides, sound and light effects etc. Not suitable for the very young.

## Caves

The ice caves of the Salzkammergut (► 17) also offer exciting adventure for children with spectacular stalactite formations, frozen waterfalls etc. Getting there is part of the fun!

## Castles & Palaces

Austria has a huge number of ruined castles, often in dramatic settings which can be fun to explore, for example Hochosterwitz in the Gurktal (► 73). Palaces and stately homes often have more to offer than just stately apartments. At Vienna's **Schönbrunn Palace**, the child-centred attractions include the Tiergarten (zoo) – said to be the world's oldest, with regularly updated displays as well as the original baroque animal houses; the Marionettentheater (Puppet Theatre), with shows including *Aladdin* and the *Magic Flute*; and the Carriage Museum. There's also a swimming pool and a children's playground.

✉ Schönbrunner Schlossstrasse 47 ☎ 81113. Puppet Theatre 817 3247 🕐 Coach Museum 9–6:30; Zoo 9–6:30 (summer), 9–sunset (winter); Park 6–sunset; Puppet Theatre ticket office Wed–Sun 3

## Museums

### Haus der Natur

Huge museum complex, with a large aquarium, reptile house, space hall and special exhibitions on mineralogy, geology etc.

✉ Museumsplatz 5, Salzburg
☎ 0662 842653 🕐 9–5
✋ Moderate

### Styrassic Park

Life-sized dinosaur models, eggs and so on in wooded parkland. Children's play area and restaurant.

✉ Dinoplatz 1, Bad Gleichenberg, nr Graz
☎ 03159 287511 🕐 Apr–Sep 8–6; Oct–Mar 9–4
✋ Moderate

### Vienna Clock Museum

More than 3,000 timepieces, including clocks in the guise of bicycles, soldiers on horseback, ballet dancers, etc (► 33).

## Theatre

### Marionettentheater

These puppet performances of famous operas (also well-known pieces like *The Nutcracker* and *Peter and the Wolf*) are an enjoyable way of introducing classical music to children over 7.

✉ Schwarzstrasse 24, Salzburg ☎ 0662 872406
🕐 Box office Mon–Sat 9–1 and 2 hours before each performance. Tickets also on sale at hotels

## Rides

Austria is one of the best countries in Europe for fun ways of getting you from A to B. Cog railways, funiculars, cable cars, chairlifts, ferries – you name it. It's also worth keeping your eye out for brochures advertising steam railways which operate at the height of the tourist season at various locations throughout the country. Check with the local tourist office for details.

# Bars, Nightclubs & Casinos

***Zum Wohl!* (Cheers!)**
Austrian beers may not be as well known as their German counterparts, but they're of a similarly high quality. Most are light lager-type beers usually available on draft (*vom Fass*). Well-known brands include *Gold Fassl* (Vienna) and *Grösser* (Styria). *Weissbier* is also good but extremely frothy. If you're a spirit drinker look out for *Obstler*, schnapps available in a variety of fruit flavours.

## Graz
### Café Harrach
Student pub near the university with a relaxed atmosphere. Snacks available.
✉ **Harrachgasse 24** ☎ **0316 322671**

### Casino Graz
French and American roulette, blackjack, baccarat and punto banco. Passport required.
✉ **Landhausgasse 10**
☎ **0316 832578** 🕐 **Daily from 3PM**

### Jedermann
Jazz and funk café with in-house DJs. Livens up around 11PM.
✉ **Leonhardgasse 3** ☎ **0316 381368**

### M1
Striking blue glass building by architect Richard Ellmer. The bars are on the upper floors from where there are fine views of the city. Twenty-something clientele.
✉ **Färberplatz** ☎ **0316 811233** 🕐 **Daily until late**

## Innsbruck
### Café Brasil
Stylishly genteel surroundings are the hallmark of this popular café-bar.
✉ **Leopoldstrasse 7** ☎ **0512 5832466**

### Filou
Haunt of the 'beautiful people', this disco-bar has a pleasant garden which closes at 10PM.
✉ **Stiftgasse 12** ☎ **0512 580256**

## Salzburg
### Augustiner Bräustube
A short, pleasant walk from the town centre (on the slopes of the Mönchberg), this bar is popular with students, locals and tourists alike. The beer is brewed on the premises.
✉ **Augustinergasse 4–6**
☎ **0662 431246** 🕐 **From 3PM, 2:30PM at weekends**

### Casino Salzburg
Try your luck at French and American roulette, blackjack, poker, red dog, seven eleven; also slot machines. Don't forget your passport.
✉ **Schloss Klessheim**
☎ **0662 845 656** 🕐 **Daily from 3PM** 🚌 **Shuttle service from town centre**

### Salamadschi
Friendly bar with modern decor by the Alter Markt.
✉ **Judengasse 10** ☎ **0662 849547** 🕐 **Daily until 2AM. Closed Sun AM**

### Vis-à-vis
Trendy cavern-like bar overlooking the Salzach.
✉ **Rudolfskai/Judengasse 13**
☎ **0662 841290** 🕐 **7PM–3AM**

## Vienna
### American Bar Kärntner
Late night watering hole with interior design by Secessionist artist Adolf Loos.
✉ **Kärntner Durchgang (off Kärntnerstrasse 10)** ☎ **512 3283** 🕐 **Sun–Thu 6PM–2AM, Fri–Sat 7PM–4AM**
🚇 **Stephansplatz**

### BACH
Worth the trek if you're into alternative music. Occasional live bands.
✉ **Bachgasse 21** ☎ **480 1953** 🕐 **Sun–Thu 8PM–2AM, Fri–Sat 8PM–4AM** 🚌 **46 from U–Bahn Thaliastrasse**

### Bettelstudent
The 'Hard-up Student' caters predominantly for a T-shirt-and-jeans crowd. Snacks are available lunchtimes and evenings and there's a good pub atmosphere, especially at weekends.
✉ Johannesgasse 12 ☎ 513 2044 🕐 Until late (3AM Sat) 🚇 Stadtpark

### Casino Wien
Gamble the night away in suitably palatial surroundings (roulette and blackjack etc).
✉ Kärntnerstrasse 41 ☎ 512 4836 🕐 Daily from 3PM

### Flex
One of the grooviest clubs in the city, featuring top DJs, live gigs and all the latest sounds.
✉ Donaukanal ☎ 512 4836 🕐 Daily 8PM–4AM 🚇 Schottenring

### Jazzland
Popular trad-jazz scene in a Bermuda Triangle cellar (near the Ruprechtskirche).
✉ Franz-Josefs-Kai 29 ☎ 533 2575 🕐 Tue–Sat 7PM–2AM 🚇 Schwedenplatz

### Krah-Krah
Busy bar in the Bermuda Triangle with snacks and an excellent choice of draft beers.
✉ Rabensteig 8 ☎ 533 8193 🕐 Mon–Sat 11AM–2AM, Sun and holidays 11AM–1AM 🚇 Schwedenplatz

### Kruger's
American-style bar where the bartenders can rustle up more than 170 cocktails and other alcoholic concoctions.
✉ Krugerstrasse 5 ☎ 512 2455 🕐 Mon–Sat 5PM–4AM, happy hour Mon–Sat 5PM–8PM

### Narrenkastle
A favourite meeting point with students, this relaxed, friendly bar also sells snacks, including baguettes, soups, salads etc.
✉ Albertgasse 12 ☎ 407 4125 🕐 Daily 5PM–2AM (Sat till 4AM)

### Roter Engel
The 'Red Angel' advertises itself as a 'song and wine bar'. It's stylish and there's often live music on offer – jazz, soul, funk, you name it.
✉ Rabensteig 5 ☎ 535 4105 🕐 Mon–Sat 5PM–4AM 🚇 Schwedenplatz

### Szene Wien
Rock music for the committed with occasional live gigs. Dress down.
✉ Hauffgasse 26 ☎ 749 3341 🕐 6PM–late 🚌 71 to Kopalgasse

### U4
Large nightclub with theme nights, eg gay night (Thu), flower power (Sun), La Notter Italiana (Mon).
✉ Schönbrunnerstrasse 222 ☎ 815 8307 🕐 Daily 10PM–5AM 🚇 Meidling Hauptstrasse

### Volksgarten
Pleasant setting with an open-air dance floor in summer. Youngish crowd.
✉ Burgring 1 ☎ 533 2105 🕐 Sun–Thu 8PM–2AM, Fri–Sat 8PM–4AM 🚌 1, 2

### Vulcania
Bermuda Triangle bar with a great selection of foreign wines and beers.
✉ Judengasse 11 ☎ 533 5905 🕐 Mon–Thu, Sun 5PM–2AM, Fri–Sat 5PM–4AM 🚇 Schwedenplatz

### Bermuda Triangles
Visitors to Vienna will soon become familiar with the *Bermuda Dreieck* (Bermuda Triangle), the area centring on Ruprechtsplatz, Rabensteig and Seitenstettengasse. A child of the 1980s, this cluster of late-night bars, restaurants and clubs really comes to life at weekends, when many of the nightspots are full to overflowing. Latterly, Graz has also acquired a Bermuda Triangle in the old town around Färbergasse, near the Hauptplatz.

# Classical Music & Theatre

## Wiener Sängerknaben

The Vienna Boys Choir was founded in 1498 by Emperor Maximilian I and, apart from the short period 1918–24, has performed since then at services in the Imperial Chapel. Two famous composers, Hadyn and Schubert, were Vienna choir boys although they would not have worn the distinctive sailors uniforms which came much later. Even if you're lucky enough to have reservations for the Sunday 9:15 mass, you won't actually see the singers in the choir gallery.

## Eisenstadt
### Schloss Esterházy

The most important event here is the annual international Haydn Festival in September. There are also weekend performances of Haydn's music at the palace during the summer.

✉ Esterházy Platz ☎ 02682 719 3000 ☎ Festival tickets: 02682 618660

## Graz

For information and ticket reservations for Graz's two major festivals, Styriarte and Steirische Herbst (Styrian Autumn), write to the address below. Styriarte takes place from late-June to mid-July and attracts international classical musicians from all over the world, as well as local Nikolaus Harnoncourt (➤ 116, panel) and his various orchestras. Styrian Autumn is an avant-garde festival of theatre, music, dance, jazz and film.

✉ Palais Attems, Sackstrasse 17, A-8010 ☎ 0316 812941

### Opera Haus (Opera House)

A varied programme of opera and ballet is staged in this grandiose 19th-century building. Some of the productions are quite progressive and tickets are fairly easy to come by throughout the season.

✉ Kaiser-Josef-Platz 1 ☎ 0316 8000

## Innsbruck
### Tiroler Landestheater

The provincial theatre stages classical operas (Mozart, Verdi etc) as well as operettas and musicals.

✉ Rennweg 2 ☎ 0512 520744

## Salzburg
### Hohensalzburg (➤ 67)

Concerts are held in the fortress throughout the year – come for chamber music, or Advent and Christmas concerts, in the state apartments.

✉ Salzburg ☎ 0662 825858 (event organiser)

### Marionettentheater

Popular operas and ballets performed by string puppets. (➤ 109).

✉ Schwarzstrasse 24 ☎ 0662 872406

### Mozarteum

Although primarily a research centre, the Mozarteum is also the venue of the Mozart Week festival in January and of other concerts throughout the season.

✉ Schwarzstrasse 26 ☎ 0662 88940-21

### Salzburger Festspiele (Salzburg Festival)

The Salzburg Festival takes place every year from the last week in July to the end of August. The concerts include opera, orchestral music and theatre, and always includes a performance of Jedermann (Everyman) by Hugo von Hofmannsthal in front of the Cathedral. Tickets are at a premium and you must book in advance by writing to the address below (also for programme details). Alternatively, you can obtain tickets for Salzburg events by emailing: ticket.shop@salzburg.co.at or ticket.service@salzburg.co.at

✉ Kartenbüro der Salzburger Festspiele, Postfach 140 A-5020 ☎ 0662 844501

## Schloss Mirabell
The emphasis here is on chamber music, especially, though not exclusively, works by Mozart.
✉ Off Marktplatz +0662 8485-86

## Vienna
### Bösendorfer Saal
Named after Vienna's most celebrated dynasty of piano makers, this is a popular venue for chamber music concerts.
✉ Graf-Starhemberg-Gasse 14 ☎ 504 6651 🚇 Taubstummengasse

### Burgkapelle
This is where the Vienna Boys Choir (▶ 112 panel) and members of the chorus and orchestra of the Vienna State Opera sing mass on Sunday mornings (9:15) from Jan–late-Jun and mid-Sep–Christmas. For tickets, write at least 10 weeks in advance to:
✉ Hofmusikkapelle Hofburg, Vienna A-1010 ☎ 533 992775 🚇 Stephansdom

### Burgtheater
This theatre is generally regarded as the flagship of Austrian drama, and the plays are in German. Even if you don't see a play, it's worth visiting the theatre for the Gustav and Ernst Klimt frescoes.
✉ Dr-Karl-Lueger-Ring 2 ☎ 514 442959 🚋 Tram 1, 2, to Burgtheater, Rathaus

### Konzerthaus
There are three halls in this august building where you can attend classical music concerts.
✉ Lothringerstrasse 20 ☎ 712 1211 🚇 Karlsplatz

### Kursalon
This is the main venue for Strauss programmes and other popular concerts.
✉ Johannesgasse 33 ☎ 713 2181 🚇 Stadtpark

### Musikverein
Very much a Viennese institution, the Musikverein has two concert halls: the Grosser Saal, home of the Vienna Philharmonic Orchestra, and the Brahmssaal (used mainly for chamber music).
✉ Dumbastrasse 3 ☎ 505 8190 🚇 Karlsplatz

### Staatsoper (State Opera)
One of the world's leading opera stages with a mainly conservative repertoire (Mozart, Verdi etc). Difficult to get tickets.
✉ Opernring 2 ☎ 514 442958 🚇 Oper

### Vienna's English Theatre
Mainstream drama from Britain and the US in English.
✉ Josefsgasse 12 ☎ 402 1260 🚇 Lerchenfelderstrasse

### Volksoper
By no means second fiddle to the more illustrious Staatsoper, the programmes at this opera house are often more adventurous, better performed and cheaper.
✉ Währinger Strasse 78 ☎ 514 443318 🚇 Volksoper

### Wiener Kammeroper
The Viennese Chamber Opera is where many of the shining lights of the Volksoper and Staatsoper start out. The programme includes many lesser-known operas, sometimes abridged.
✉ Fleischmarkt 24 ☎ 513 6072 🚇 Schwedenplatz

### Bregenz Festspiele
One of Austria's most spectacular theatrical settings is the floating stage on Bodensee (Lake Constance), which features in the annual Bregenzer Festival. The capacity audience of 6,000 is seated on land in a 30-tier amphitheatre. Productions include mainly grand opera but also operettas and musical comedies. In the 1999 production of Verdi's *Un Ballo in Maschera* (Masked Ball), the chorus was disgorged onto the set from a floating coffin to people the pages of a gigantic book held open by a 15m-high skeleton.

113

# Sport & Leisure

**Bobsleigh**

Innsbruck has hosted the Winter Olympics twice – in 1964 and 1976 – and as a result the sporting facilities here are second to none. However, you don't need to be a professional athlete to enjoy the thrills of the bobsleigh. From May–Oct, Thu–Sun at 4PM, you can hurtle down the Olympic Bobsleigh run. Contact Sommerbob
☎ 0512 377160

## Cycling

Austria has more than 8,000km of marked and well-signposted cycle routes. The Austrian National Tourist Office publishes a leaflet, *Cycling in Austria,* listing tour operators offering cycling holidays. Any regional tourist office will provide brochures and maps as well as information about bike hire. One of the best areas for unstrenuous cycling is Burgenland – the Eisenstadt office has a wealth of material to help you plan itineraries.

For cycling tours of Vienna contact **Pedal Power**. The daily guided bike tours take place regardless of the weather and last about three hours, taking in the major sights, with plenty of photo stops. The tours start at the entrance to the ferris wheel. Bike rental (for adults and children) is also available.
✉ **Ausstellungsstrasse 3, Vienna** ☎ **729 7234, fax 729 7235** 🚇 **Praterstern**

## Fishing

Austria's rivers and lakes are made for fishing, but first you'll need to buy a licence (daily or weekly) . Contact the local tourist office to find out how to buy one and for information about sports shops, where to fish, rules and regulations etc.
For more information contact:

**Fishing Ground Austria**
✉ **Hauptstrasse 203, A-9210 Pörtschach** ☎ **0472 362040, fax 0472 36 20 90, email fischwasser@stw.co.at**

## Golf

There are currently more than 100 golf courses in Austria and the number is growing all the time. One of the great advantages of golfing here, of course, is the magnificent scenery. For locations ask the National Tourist Office for the booklet *Courses and Hotels in Austria* or contact:

**Österreichischer Golf-Verband**
✉ **Prinz-Eugen-Strasse 12, Haus des Sports, A-1040 Wien** ☎ **01 505 3245**

## Paragliding & Hangliding

This adventure activity is becoming increasingly popular in Austria. The minimum age is 16 years. There are schools in Seeboden (Carinthia); Mattsee and Salzburg (Salzburger Land); Graz and Ramsau am Dachstein (Styria); Galtur, Ötztal, Leinz and Neustift (Tirol); and Leonstein, Linz and Spital in Upper Austria.

## Skiing and Winter Sports

There are ski resorts throughout alpine Austria, but the best known are Lech and St Anton (► 84–5) in the Arlberg massif, Kitzbühel (► 20) in the Tirol and St Johann in Salzburger Land. The season generally runs from Nov to Apr, depending on conditions. There are slopes for all abilities and most resorts have ski schools. Snow-boarding is also increasingly popular. For days off piste, the larger towns also offer skating rinks, indoor swimming pools and horse-drawn sleigh rides.

## Summer in the Alps

Though famous for skiing and other winter sports, the Austrian Alps are year-round sporting destinations. Check out the following:
Mountain biking – St Anton.
Mountaineering and rock climbing – Ötzal, Kaprun and Mayrhofen (school for beginners).
Riding – horse trekking for all abilities is available at many summer resorts. Full information on riding in Austria can be obtained from:

**Horseback Riding in Austria:**
✉ Mairhof 4–5, A-4121 Altenfelden ☎ 07282 5952, fax 07282 59232, email reitarena@upperaustria. or.at

Summer tobogganning – Saalfelden (near Zell am See) and St Johann (Tirol).
Summer glacier skiing – Hintertux (Zillertal), Kaprun and Sölden

## Walking

Austria is one of the best countries in Europe for walking and hiking. Most of the hills and mountain areas have well-marked paths and signposts indicating distance and duration. Make sure you take the proper clothing and footwear with you and, especially where hiking is concerned, let someone in authority know where you're heading off to. If you're planning on a mountain walking holiday, it might be worth joining the Austrian Alpine Club:
✉ Österreichischer Alpenverein, Wilhelm-Griel-Strasse 15, Innsbruck ☎ 0512

59547 (members receive a 50 percent reduction on accommodation in alpine huts run by the ÖAV).
Most regional tourist authorities have brochures detailing walking opportunities to suit all abilities in their area. For those who fancy a trek with someone else carrying all the baggage then a tour with porterage is ideal. Try the seven-day Danube Hillside Route, where you walk along the Danube every day and arrive at a comfortable hotel every evening, where your luggage will be waiting. Contact:

**Oberösterreich Touristik GmbH**
✉ Postfach 15.000, A-4021 Linz
☎ 0732 773024, fax 0732 773025, email info@touristik.at

## Watersports

The best centres for windsurfing and sailing are the Salzkammergut lakes, Wörther See (➤ 22), Millstättersee, Neusiedler See (➤ 60), Attersee in Salzburger Land and Bodensee.
Water skiing and paraskiing are possible, though less widely available. Canoeing, kayaking and river rafting (May to Oct only) are popular on river locations in the Tirol, including Mayrhofen, Taxenbach and Sölden.
Most of the lakeside resorts have beaches, that is, grassy bathing areas with diving boards and other facilities. The water in many of Austria's lakes is warmer than you might expect, especially the Wörther See, where swimming in May is the norm.

### Austrian Greats

Austria has produced more than its fair share of skiing champions. Anyone over forty will remember Franz Klammer's famous victory in the men's downhill in the 1976 Winter Olympics in Innsbruck. Annemarie Moser-Pröll won an astonishing 62 World Cup events, an all-time record. Petra Kronberger, besides being a double Olympic gold medallist in Albertville, was the first female skier to appear on the cover of *Time* magazine.

# What's On When

### Musical Aristocrat

Now aged 70, Nikolaus Harnoncourt has won world renown as an interpreter of Mozart and an expert on period instrument performances. Born in Berlin, the great-great grandson of an archduke, he established his reputation in the 1970s. Although Graz remains his 'home base', he is a familiar figure on opera stages around the world and also appears regularly at the Vienna festival.

### January

*New Year's Day Concert* performed by the Vienna Philharmonic Orchestra in the Musikverein.
*Mozartwoche* (Mozart Week), one of Salzburg's many celebrations of the great composer's music.

### February

*Fasching* (Carnival) culminates in the Shrove Tuesday festivities all over the country.

### Mid-April to mid-May

*Bregenz Spring Festival* of music and dance.

### May–mid to June

*Wiener Festwochen* (Vienna Festival): Opera, music, theatre and film.

### Mid-May to late October

Concerts of music by Haydn, in Schloss Esterházy, Eisenstadt, culminating in *International Hadyn Festival*.

### June

*Corpus Christi* in the Salzkammergut towns of Ebensee, Traunsee and Hallstatt, with flower-bedecked barge processions on the lakes.
*Danube Island Festival*: Mega-party which in the past has attracted internationally known bands.

### Mid-June to mid-July

*Styriarte*: The Graz festival of classical music under Nikolaus Harnoncourt.

### July to mid-September

*Klangbogen Wien*, Vienna's Music Festival of grand opera, chamber music, orchestral concerts. Includes two weeks of jazz in July.

### July–August

Music concerts in Schloss Ambras, Innsbruck, culminating in the *Festival of Old Music*.
*Bad Ischl* operetta weeks.
*Open-air Operetta Festival* in Mörbisch, Neusiedler See.
*International Musikwoche*: Millstatt's chamber music festival.
*Bregenz Festival*: classical opera on a floating stage on the Bodensee.
*Salzburg International Festival* of opera and music.

### September–October

*The International Bruckner Festival* in Linz opens with fireworks and includes theatre and art exhibitions as well as concerts.
*Styrian Autumn Festival* in Graz introduces avant-garde music, film, art and theatre.

### Late October

*'Viennale' film festival*: including experimental films.
*Wien Modern*, a festival of contemporary classical music.

### November

*Salzburger Jazz Herbst*: international and local groups.

### December

*Christmas markets* are held in the cities. Innsbruck marks St Nicholas' Day (6 Dec) with a procession.
On Christmas Eve, the places to be are the chapel at Oberndorf, near Salzburg, which holds a service which includes the singing of Silent Night, composed by local organist, Franz Gruber; and St Stephen's Cathedral, Vienna, where midnight mass is a social event – you'll need to get an entrance pass in advance.

# Practical Matters

Above: *Tram in Maria-Theresien-Strasse, Innsbruck*
Right: *Vienna bus stop*

## TIME DIFFERENCES

| GMT 12 noon | Austria 1PM | Germany 1PM | USA (NY) 7AM | Netherlands 1PM | Spain 1PM |
|---|---|---|---|---|---|

**GMT** 12 noon → **Austria** 1PM → **Germany** 1PM ← **USA (NY)** 7AM → **Netherlands** 1PM → **Spain** 1PM

## BEFORE YOU GO

### WHAT YOU NEED

● Required
○ Suggested
▲ Not required

| | UK | Germany | USA | Netherlands | Spain |
|---|---|---|---|---|---|
| Passport | ● | ● | ● | ● | ● |
| Visa | ▲ | ▲ | ▲ | ▲ | ▲ |
| Onward or Return Ticket | ▲ | ▲ | ▲ | ▲ | ▲ |
| Health Inoculations | ▲ | ▲ | ▲ | ▲ | ▲ |
| Health Documentation (► 123, Health) | ○ | ○ | ○ | ○ | ○ |
| Travel Insurance | ○ | ○ | ○ | ○ | ○ |
| Driving Licence (national with German translation or International) | ● | ● | ● | ● | ● |
| Car Insurance Certificate (if own car) | ● | ● | ● | ● | ● |
| Car Registration Document (if own car) | ● | ● | ● | ● | ● |

### WHEN TO GO

**Vienna**

High season

Low season

| 1°C | 3°C | 9°C | 15°C | 19°C | 23°C | 26°C | 25°C | 20°C | 15°C | 7°C | 4°C |
|---|---|---|---|---|---|---|---|---|---|---|---|
| JAN | FEB | MAR | APR | MAY | JUN | JUL | AUG | SEP | OCT | NOV | DEC |
| ❄ | ❄ | ❄ | 🌧 | 🌤 | 🌤 | ☀ | ☀ | ☀ | 🌧 | 🌧 | ❄ |

🌧 Wet    ☀ Sun    🌤 Sun/showers    ❄ Snow

### TOURIST OFFICES

In the UK
30 St George Street
London
W1R OAL
☎ 020 7629 0461
Fax: 020 7499 6038

In the USA
500, Fifth Avenue
Suite 2009-22
New York
NY 10110
☎ 212 944 6885
Fax: 212 730 4568

11601 Wilshire Blvd.
Suite 2480
Los Angeles
California 90025
☎ 310 477 3332
Fax 310 477 5141

**POLICE 133**

**FIRE 122**

**AMBULANCE 144**

## WHEN YOU ARE THERE

### ARRIVING

The major international airports are Salzburg and Vienna. The domestic air companies are Austrian Airlines, Lauda Air and Tyrolean Airways. Austrian Federal Railways (ÖBB) runs a reliable and frequent service which links Austria to all European countries.

| Vienna | Journey times |
|--------|---------------|
| Flughafen Wien-Schwechat to Wien-Mitte South-east, S-Bahn line S7 |  25 minutes |
| | 25 minutes |
| **20 kilometres** | 25 minutes |

| Salzburg   west | Journey times |
|-----------------|---------------|
| Bus 77 to Südtirolerplatz | 15 minutes |
| | 15 minutes |
| **3 kilometres** | 15 minutes |

### TIME

 Austria is on Central European Time, one hour ahead of GMT, 6 hours ahead of New York and 9 hours behind Sydney.

### MONEY

The unit of currency is the Austrian Schilling (AS) denominated in notes of 20, 50, 100, 500, 1000 and 5000 and in coins of 1, 5, 10 and 20. The Groschen (.01 of a Schilling) is worth very little and rarely encountered. Credit cards (Visa, Mastercard and Diner's Club) are accepted by the larger hotels, restaurants and some garages but smaller establishments prefer cash, some refusing to take cards altogether.

ATMs for cash advances can be found outside banks in all the major towns. The euro will start circulation on 1 January 2002, with the Schilling due to be phased out on 1 July 2002.

### CUSTOMS

 **YES**
**From another EU country for personal use (guidelines):**
800 cigarettes, 200 cigars, 1 kilogram of tobacco
10 litres of spirits (over 22%)
20 litres of aperitifs
90 litres of wine, of which 60 litres can be sparkling wine
110 litres of beer

**From a non-EU country for your personal use, the allowances are:**
200 cigarettes OR
50 cigars OR 250 grams of tobacco
1 litre of spirits (over 22%)
2 litres of fortified wine (e.g. sherry), sparkling wine or other liqueurs
2 litres of still wine
50 ml of perfume
250ml of eau de toilette
The value limit for goods is 175 euros.

**Travellers under 17 years of age are not entitled to the tobacco and alcohol allowances.**

 **NO**
Drugs, firearms, ammunition, offensive weapons, obscene material, unlicensed animals.

## CONSULATES

USA
01 313391

UK
01 716 135151

Germany
01 71154-0

Netherlands
01 589 39215

Spain
01 505 578

## WHEN YOU ARE THERE

### TOURIST OFFICES

Every town and village has its own tourist office which provides maps and brochures. They do not book accommodation but will direct you to a hotel booking agent.
**Austrian National Tourist Board** www.anto.com

**Regional Offices:**

**Vienna**
● Obere Augartenstrasse 40
A-1025 Wien
☎ 01 211 144
Fax: 01 216 8492
www.info.wien.at

**Carinthia (Kärnten)**
● Casinoplatz 1
A-9220 Velden
☎ 04274 52100
Fax: 04274 52100-50
www.tiscover.com/carinthia

**Salzburger Land**
● Postfach 1
Hallwang bei Salzburg
A-5033 Salzburg
☎ 0662 66880
Fax: 0662 6688-0
www.sagma.co.at/guide

**Styria (Steiermark)**
● St Peter Hauptstrasse 293
A-8042 Graz
☎ 0316 403033-0
Fax: 0316 403033-10
www.steiermark.com

**Tirol**
● Wilhelm-Greil-Strasse 17
A-6010 Innsbruck
☎ 0512 5320-170
Fax: 0512 5320-174
www.tis.co.at/tirol

**Vorarlberg**
● Bahnhofstrasse 14
A-6900 Bregenz
☎ 05574 42525-0
Fax: 05574 42525-5
www.vol.at/tourismus

### NATIONAL HOLIDAYS

| J | F | M | A | M | J | J | A | S | O | N | D |
|---|---|---|---|---|---|---|---|---|---|---|---|
| 2 |   |   | 1 | 2 | 2 |   | 1 |   |   | 1 | 3 |

1 Jan     New Year's Day
6 Jan     Epiphany
Easter Monday
1 May     Labour Day
Ascension Day 6th Thu after Easter
Whit Monday 6th Mon after Easter
Corpus Christi
15 Aug    Assumption Day
26 Oct    National Day)
1 Nov     All Saints' Day
8 Dec     Immaculate Conception
25 Dec    Christmas Day
26 Dec    St Stephen's Day

### OPENING HOURS

○ Shops        ● Museums
● Offices      ● Post Offices
● Banks        ● Pharmacies

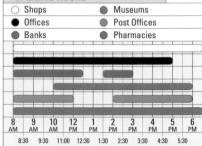

| 8 AM | 9 AM | 10 AM | 12 PM | 1 PM | 2 PM | 3 PM | 4 PM | 5 PM | 6 PM |
|------|------|-------|-------|------|------|------|------|------|------|
| 8:30 | 9:30 | 11:00 | 12:30 | 1:30 | 2:30 | 3:30 | 4:30 | 5:30 | |

Most shops take a 1–2-hour lunch break and open Sat 8AM–1PM. In Vienna banks stay open until 5:30 on Thursdays. Museums open Sat–Sun 9AM–6PM, and 9AM–4PM in winter. Many museums in Vienna and Salzburg close Mondays, other days in other places. Check in advance with the tourist office. Pharmacies operate a rota system to provide a 24-hour service – details are posted on the shop doors.
On national holidays banks, offices and most shops close. However, restaurants, museums and other tourist attractions tend to stay open, some with restricted hours. (On National Day you will find that many museums are free.)

**DRIVE ON THE
RIGHT**

**TOILETS
CHARGE**

★★
★☆

## PUBLIC TRANSPORT

**Internal Flights**
Austrian Air Services operate flights between Graz, Innsbruck, Klagenfurt, Linz, Salzburg and Vienna. Tyrolean Airways fly from Innsbruck.

Austrian Federal Railways – Österreichische Bundesbahnen (ÖBB) – run efficient, comfort-able services throughout the country, covering the main towns and many remarkably scenic routes. Some long distance trains have women-only compartments and children's playpens (check the timetables for details). Inter-City (IC) and Euro-City (EC) trains carry a supplement, included in the price of the ticket. Austria also has cog railways and many narrow gauge tracks – a few offering steam train excursions during the summer. For more information contact ÖBB, Bahn-Totalservice, Wien Westbahnhof ☎ 01 580 032200.

**Trams/buses**
Austria has a good network of bus and coach services, which are cheaper than trains and cover outlying areas, but of course take longer. Vienna, Graz and Innsbruck have trams as well as buses.

**Boats**
Danube boats carry passengers between Passau, Vienna and Budapest (Apr–Oct). ÖBB operate routes on the Danube and ferries on the Bodensee and Wolfgangsee, while private companies ferry passengers on the other lakes.

**Metro**
Vienna has a fast and efficient 5-line U-Bahn and rapid transit commuter trains (S-Bahn) which connect the suburbs and the airport.

## CAR RENTAL

Renting cars in Austria is quite expensive and it's usually cheaper to book from home. Major car rental companies have branches in most towns and at airports. An Austrian agency is: Autoverleih Buchbinder ✉ Schlachthausgasse 38, Vienna ☎ 01 717 50-0.

## TAXIS

Fares are metred and taxis are not unreasonably expensive. In Vienna, expect to pay surcharges for luggage, for Sundays and bank holidays, for trips to the airport and after 11PM.

## DRIVING

Speed limit on motorways: **130kph.** Toll payable – cars must display sticker (Pickerl) before using the motorway

Speed limit on trunk roads: **100kph**

Speed limit on urban roads: **50km**; in some towns special **20km** limits apply.

Seatbelts, back and front, are compulsory. Children under 12 may not ride in the front.

Don't drink alcohol before driving. The limit is practically zero (0.5 parts per thousand).

All petrol is unleaded – 91-octane regular, 95-octane super and diesel. Prices are uniform throughout the country, but petrol stations close on Sundays in rural areas.

The Österreichischer Automobile, Motorrad und Touring Club (ÖAMTC) ☎ 120 and the Auto-, Motor- und Radfahrerbund Österreichs (ARBÖ) ☎ 123, both operate breakdown callout services and accept AA and RAC insurance cover.

CENTIMETRES

INCHES

## PERSONAL SAFETY

Austria is among the safest countries in Europe from the traveller's point of view, but it's sensible to take the usual precautions especially on public transport.

- Watch your bag in tourist areas.
- Never leave anything of value on show in your car.
- Deposit your valuables in the hotel safe.
- Avoid walking alone at night.

Police assistance:
☎ **133**

## ELECTRICITY

Electric current is 220 volts AC and appliances need two-round-pin continental plugs.

## TELEPHONES

Austrian phone booths are generally dark green with yellow roofs. All boxes, even the new glass ones, display the post horn symbol. Most boxes will only accept phone cards which are sold by post offices

and tobacconists.

You may see local numbers followed by a hyphen and a couple of extra digits – this is the extension and can be called direct.

**International Dialling Codes**

From Austria to:

| UK: 00 44 |
| --- |
| Germany: 00 49 |
| USA and Canada: 00 1 |
| Netherlands: 00 31 |
| France: 00 33 |
| International operator: 1616 |
| Directory enquiries: 1613 |
| Local directory enquiries: 1611 |

## POST

Postage stamps are sold at post offices and from tobacco kiosks. Post boxes are yellow. Post Office (*Postamt*) opening times are generally Mon–Fri 8–12, 2–6. In major cities hours extend through lunch time and into Saturday morning and at least one office will be open 24 hours. *Poste restante* letters can be sent to any post office.

## TIPS/GRATUITIES

| Yes ✓   No ✗ | | |
| --- | --- | --- |
| Hotel | ✓ | 10 AS |
| Restaurants (round up bill) | ✓ | 5–7% |
| Cafés (round up bill) | ✓ | 5–50 AS |
| Taxis (5–10 AS) | ✓ | 10% |
| Tour guides | ✓ | 20 AS |
| Porters | ✓ | 10 AS |
| Usherettes | ✗ | none |
| Hairdressers | ✓ | 5% |
| Cloakroom attendants | ✓ | 10 AS |
| Toilets | ✓ | 2–5 AS |

## PHOTOGRAPHY

**When to photograph**: There's no shortage of subjects in this picture-postcard country

**Best times to photograph**: the summer sun can be too bright at the height of the day making photos taken at this time appear 'flat'. It is best to take photographs in the early morning or late evening.

**Where to buy film**: Film and camera equipment is available as in other European countries.

## HEALTH

**Insurance**
Citizens of the EU receive free hospital treatment on production of their passport. Nationals of other countries should check beforehand whether there's a reciprocal health agreement with Austria. Private medical insurance is advised (essential for non-EU visitors).

**Dental Services**
If you require urgent treatment, there is an emergency dental helpline in Vienna:
Emergency Dentist ☎ 5122078

**Sun Advice**
The sun is not a real problem in Austria. Take the usual precautions especially during the sunniest months, June, July and August and when on the ski slopes.

**Drugs**
Pharmacies (*Apotheken*) are the only places that sell over-the-counter medicines. Take all prescription medicines with you.

**Safe Water**
Tap water throughout Austria is safe for drinking. Bottled water is also available from Austrian springs – look out for well-known brands *Vöslauer* and *Römerquelle*.

## CONCESSIONS

**Students** Holders of an International Student Identity Card (ISIC) are entitled to reductions in museums and other attractions. The Eurail pass is valid on Austrian trains. There are two Youth Hostelling Associations:
Österreichischer Jugendherbergsverband
✉ Schottenring 28, Vienna ☎ 0222 533 5353;
Österreichisches Jugendherbergswerk
✉ Helferstorferstrasse 4, Vienna ☎ 0222 533 1833.
**Senior Citizens** The best policy is to mention at the outset that you're a senior citizen when making reservations, buying tickets etc. Some museums offer concessions. ÖBB offer a Seniorenpass for discounted rail travel (you will need a photograph and identification). When renting a car, ask for promotional discounts to senior citizens.

## CLOTHING SIZES

| Austria | UK | Rest of Europe | USA | | |
|---|---|---|---|---|---|
| 46 | 36 | 46 | 36 | | Suits |
| 48 | 38 | 48 | 38 | | |
| 50 | 40 | 50 | 40 | | |
| 52 | 42 | 52 | 42 | | |
| 54 | 44 | 54 | 44 | | |
| 56 | 46 | 56 | 46 | | |
| 41 | 7 | 41 | 8 | | Shoes |
| 42 | 7.5 | 42 | 9 | | |
| 43 | 8.5 | 43 | 10 | | |
| 44 | 9.5 | 44 | 11 | | |
| 45 | 10.5 | 45 | 12 | | |
| 46 | 11 | 46 | 13 | | |
| 37 | 14.5 | 37 | 14.5 | | Shirts |
| 38 | 15 | 38 | 15 | | |
| 39/40 | 15.5 | 39/40 | 15.5 | | |
| 41 | 16 | 41 | 16 | | |
| 42 | 16.5 | 42 | 16.5 | | |
| 43 | 17 | 43 | 17 | | |
| 36 | 8 | 36 | 6 | | Dresses |
| 38 | 10 | 38 | 8 | | |
| 40 | 12 | 40 | 10 | | |
| 42 | 14 | 42 | 12 | | |
| 44 | 16 | 44 | 14 | | |
| 46 | 18 | 46 | 16 | | |
| 38 | 4.5 | 38 | 6 | | Shoes |
| 38 | 5 | 39 | 6.5 | | |
| 39 | 5.5 | 39 | 7 | | |
| 39 | 6 | 39 | 7.5 | | |
| 40 | 6.5 | 40 | 8 | | |
| 41 | 7 | 41 | 8.5 | | |

## WHEN DEPARTING

- Contact the airline at least 72 hours before departure to reconfirm your booking to prevent being 'bumped' from the plane because of over-allocation.
- Make sure you leave in plenty of time for your flight – allow at least 2 hours before scheduled departure time.
- The airport departure tax is normally included in the cost of the ticket

### LANGUAGE

Austria's official language is German. A quick pronunciation guide: *ä* is pronounced like English *air*, *ö* like *err*, *ü* like *oo*, *au* is *ow* (as in now), *oo* is *or*, *ie* is always *ee* and *ei* always *eye*. The character 'ß' (eg in Straße) is equivalent to 'ss'. All nouns are capitalised.

| | | | |
|---|---|---|---|
| hotel | *das Hotel* | how much?... | *wieviel kostet es?* |
| room | *das Zimmer* | breakfast | *das Frühstuck* |
| I would like a | *Ich hätte gern* | toilet | *die Toilette* |
| single | *ein Einzelzimmer* | cold/hot water | *kaltes/warmes Wasser* |
| double room | *ein Doppelzimmer* | towel | *das Handtuch* |
| | | soap | *die Seife* |
| with bath | *mit Bad* | telephone | *das Telefon* |
| with shower | *mit Dusche* | key | *der Schlüssel* |
| for one night | *für eine Nacht* | lift/elevator | *der Aufzug* |

| | | | |
|---|---|---|---|
| money | *das Geld* | too much | *zuviel* |
| bank | *die Bank* | free (no charge) | *gratis/umsonst* |
| post office | *das Postamt* | more/less | *mehr/weniger* |
| Austrian Schilling | *österreichischer Schilling* | large/small | *gross/klein* |
| | | the bill | *die Rechnung* |
| Groschen | *der Groschen* | I'd like | *Ich möchte ...* |
| credit card | *Kreditkarte* | to buy ... | *kaufen* |
| cheap | *billig* | I'd like to | *Ich möchte ...* |
| expensive | *teuer* | exchange ... | *wechseln* |

| | | | |
|---|---|---|---|
| restaurant | *das Restaurant* | table | *die Tafel* |
| Do you take credit cards? | *Darf Ich mit Kreditkarte zahlen?* | wine | *der Wein* |
| | | white/red | *weiss/rot* |
| | | water | *das Wasser* |
| coffee house | *das Kaffeehaus* | lunch | *Mittagessen* |
| pub | *die Gaststätte* | dinner | *Abendessen* |
| beer | *das Bier* | menu of the day | *Tagesmenü* |
| menu | *die Speisekarte* | waiter | *Herr Ober* |

| | | | |
|---|---|---|---|
| airport | *der Flughafen* | straight on | *geradeaus* |
| railway station | *der Bahnhof* | When does the train leave? | *Wann fährt der Zug ab?* |
| subway station | *die U-bahn-station* | | |
| | | ticket | *die Fahrkarte* |
| bus stop | *die Bushaltestelle* | return ticket | *die Rückfahrkarte* |
| bus | *der Bus* | platform | *der Bahnsteig* |
| tram | *die Strassenbahn* | arrival/departure | *Ankunft/Abfahrt* |
| right/left | *rechts/links* | non-smoking | *Nichtraucher* |

| | | | |
|---|---|---|---|
| yes | *ja* | excuse me please | *Entschuldigen Sie bitte* |
| no | *nein* | | |
| please | *bitte* | yesterday | *gestern* |
| thank you | *danke* | tomorrow | *morgen* |
| hello | *Guten Tag/ Grüss Gott* | open | *geöffnet/offen/auf* |
| | | closed | *geschlossen/zu* |
| goodbye | *Auf Wiedersehen* | where is? | *wo ist?* |
| good morning | *Guten Morgen* | here | *hier* |
| good evening | *Guten Abend* | how are you? | *wie geht es Ihnen?* |
| today | *heute* | | |

**Acknowledgements**
The Automobile Association wishes to thank the following photographers, libraries and associations for their assistance in the preparation of this book.

AUSTRIAN NATIONAL TOURIST OFFICE 1, 17b, 25b, 40b, 56b, 65b, 86; BRIDGEMAN ART LIBRARY 21b Peasant Wedding (Bauernhochzeit), 1568 (panel) by Pieter Brueghel the Elder (c.1515–69) (Kunsthistorisches Museum, Vienna, Austria), 39b The Kiss, 1907–8 by Gustav Klimt (1862–1918) (Österreichische Galerie, Vienna, Austria); BRUCE COLEMAN COLLECTION 13c, 15b; CORBIS 23c (Adam Woolfitt), 31b (Jerry Cooke), 44 (Adam Woolfitt), 49b (Massimo Listri), 55b (Adam Woolfitt), 57 (Massimo Listri), 90 (Ric Ergenbright); MARY EVANS PICTURE LIBRARY 10b; ILLUSTRATED LONDON NEWS 11b, 14c; INNSBRUCK TOURISM 59b; MRI BANKERS' GUIDE TO FOREIGN CURRENCY 119; REX FEATURES 14b (Bob Grant); C & M RICE 117b, 122a, 122b, 122c; SPECTRUM COLOUR LIBRARY 6b, 9b, 18b, 20b, 23b, 45b, 50, 52b, 59a, 64b, 69, 76b, 83b, 84a, 84b; WORLD PICTURES F/C (c), 2, 8c, 9c, 16b, 22b, 28b, 28/9, 41a, 41b, 46, 48b, 51b, 53b, 54b, 60b, 60/1, 61a, 62, 67b, 68b, 70, 71, 72/3, 73b, 75, 77, 81b, 87a, 91b, 117a;

The remaining pictures are held in the Association's own library (AA PHOTO LIBRARY) with contributions from the following photographers:

Martin Adelman 85; Adrian Baker 5b, 7b, 8b, 19b, 47, 48a, 49a, 51a, 52a, 53a, 54a, 55a, 56a, 58a, 60a, 63, 64a, 65a, 67a, 68a, 72, 73a, 74a, 74b, 76a, 78, 79, 80a, 81a, 82a, 82b, 83a, 87b, 88a, 89a, 91a, 92/116; Peter Baker F/C (b), 7c, 12b, 13b, 38b, 58b, 66, 89b; David Noble 36b, 42b; Clive Sawyer 15a, 16a, 17a, 18a, 19a, 20a, 21a, 22a, 23a, 24a, 24/5, 25a, 26a, 26b, 27b, 28a, 33c, 37b; Michael Siebert F/C (a), (d), B/C, 5a, 6a, 7a, 8a, 9a, 10a, 11a, 12a, 13a, 14a, 27a, 29a, 29b, 30a, 31a, 32a, 33a, 33b, 36a, 37a, 38a, 39a, 40a, 42a, 43a, 43b, 43c, 45a.

**Author's Acknowledgements**
Oskar Hinteregger and the staff of the Austrian Tourist Board, London; Austrian Airlines; Austrian Railways (ÖBB); local tourist offices throughout Austria for their courtesy and co-operation.

Copy editor: Anne Heseltine  Page layout: Barfoot Design

# *Dear Essential Traveller*

**Your comments, opinions and recommendations are very
important to us. So please help us to improve our travel
guides by taking a few minutes to complete this simple
questionnaire.**

*You do not need a stamp (unless posted outside the UK). If you do not want to cut this page
from your guide, then photocopy it or write your answers on a plain sheet of paper.*

*Send to:* **The Editor, AA World Travel Guides,
FREEPOST SCE 4598, Basingstoke RG21 4GY.**

## Your recommendations...

We always encourage readers' recommendations for restaurants, nightlife
or shopping – if your recommendation is used in the next edition of the
guide, we will send you a *FREE* AA *Essential* **Guide** of your choice.
Please state below the establishment name, location and your reasons
for recommending it.

_____

_____

_____

_____

Please send me **AA *Essential*** _____

   (*see list of titles inside the front cover*)

## About this guide...

Which title did you buy?

   AA *Essential* _____

Where did you buy it? _____

When? m m / y y

Why did you choose an AA *Essential* Guide? _____

_____

_____

_____

_____

Did this guide meet your expectations?

   Exceeded ☐   Met all ☐   Met most ☐   Fell below ☐

   Please give your reasons _____

_____

_____

_____

*continued on next page...*

Were there any aspects of this guide that you particularly liked? _____

_____

_____

_____

Is there anything we could have done better? _____

_____

_____

_____

_____

## About you...

Name (*Mr/Mrs/Ms*) _____

Address _____

_____

_____ Postcode _____

Daytime tel nos _____

Which age group are you in?
Under 25 ☐   25–34 ☐   35–44 ☐   45–54 ☐   55–64 ☐   65+ ☐

How many trips do you make a year?
Less than one ☐   One ☐   Two ☐   Three or more ☐

Are you an AA member? Yes ☐   No ☐

## About your trip...

When did you book? m m / y y          When did you travel? m m / y y

How long did you stay? _____

Was it for business or leisure? _____

Did you buy any other travel guides for your trip?

If yes, which ones? _____

_____

Thank you for taking the time to complete this questionnaire. Please send
it to us as soon as possible, and remember, you do not need a stamp
(*unless posted outside the UK*).

## *Happy Holidays!*